BILLY
BUTLER
M.B.E
MRS BUTLER'S ELDEST

"Billy Butler cares for his city with a great
passion and wit that is totally sincere.
He's also wonderfully generous with his time,
that is the greatest generosity of all.
Billy Butler and me sitting opposite each other –
one an optimist and the other a pessimist.
Perhaps his greatest achievement of all is that
Billy Butler ALWAYS makes me SMILE."

Alan Bleasdale

BILLY

BUTLER

M.B.E

MRS BUTLER'S ELDEST

TrinityMirror Media

Copyright: Billy Butler

Produced in 2010 by Trinity Mirror Sport Media

Business Development Director: Mark Dickinson. Executive Editor: Ken Rogers.
Senior Editor: Steve Hanrahan. Editor: Paul Dove. Senior Art Editor: Rick Cooke.

Written by Billy Butler

Book Editor: Peter Grant

Design & Production: Zoe Bevan / Vicky Andrews
Additional Resarch: Brian Johnston / Cathy Roberts

Cover design: Rick Cooke, Colin Harrison
Additional design: Zoe Bevan

ISBN: 9 781906 802530

Photographs:
Trinity Mirror, PA Pics. Billy Butler Collection

Printed by CPI Mackays, Chatham ME5 8TD

In memory of . . . me Mam

My Mum was born in 1914 and lived until she was 79.
I lived with her as part of our family until I was 22.
My memories of my mam are of her sitting playing the
guitar and singing. She learned to play the guitar by
watching my dad, who I believe was a very good guitarist
and crooner who often used to sing outside cinema queues
to make money to go for a drink.
My mum played street games with us – she made us go to
church and made sure we all dressed in our best each
Sunday. I used to watch her adding up her debts each
weekend (including money I owed her). I can never
remember her having a holiday but she took us to Moreton,
New Brighton and Freshfield whenever she could.
She never went out much and as we lived with my
Granddad he said 'it wasn't right for a widow to go out'.
Her best mate was Mrs Myers from our street.
When she took me to the pictures she always used to wipe
my mouth with her handkerchief and the smell of her
make-up on that handkerchief will remain with me forever.
We never had much but we were never aware of it. I can't
remember a Christmas when Father Xmas didn't bring me
all I asked. How my mum managed I don't know.
Me, my sisters and brother were so proud of her and I was
so proud to be called Mrs Butler's Eldest.

Not forgetting . . .

My wife Lesley for her unending patience, encouragement
and support. My sisters Joan and Dorothy for childhood
memories and my mother-in-law Darlene for her faith in me.

No one makes it alone.

Billy Butler

BILLY BUTLER'S SHOWBIZ C.V.

TV	RADIO	AWARDS
1961/62 *Thank Your Lucky Stars*, 20 Appearances including two *All Liverpool* Shows.	**1971** *Radio M*	5 *Scouseology*
		1 *Local Media Award*
	1979 *Radio City*	2, *Night Out, Top DJ Awards*
1970S *Mersey Pirate Fun factory*	**1983** *Radio M*	
1980S *Chuckle Vision* (Story Teller) *What's ON,* Granada *Reports in Wrestling and Clog Dancing* (not at the same time) *Whackers World What The Butler Sees Fax* (With Bill Oddie – three series).	**1995** *Radio City* **2000** *Radio M* (Back to my spiritual home) *I also presented *Late Night Friday Show* on Radio 2, 1986	*In 1979 came 2nd in *Daily Mirror Nation al Local Radio Top Dj Survey* (Got beat by one point on Sex Appeal) Variety Club Tribute. Sony Awards For Hold Your Plums
1990S *Billy & Wally's Big Night Out*, Channel One TV, 50 shows – all local arts.		

B I L L Y
BUTLER

CONTENTS

PILOT OF THE AIRWAVES, *by Billy Butler*	09
MRS BUTLER'S ELDEST, *by Peter Grant*	11
FIVEWORDS	15
MY MATE BILLY, *by Wally Scott*	21
BILLY THE KID	
CAVERN DAYS	33
PLUM JOBS	43
THOSE WERE THE DAYS	51
REMEMBER WHEN	59
MY BEST EVER . . .	123
OFF AIR	149
HOLD YOUR PLUMS	153
DEDICATIONS	159
OUTRO	182

Billy Butler
MBE

40 years on radio . . . 50 years in showbiz.
Welcome to an autobiography with a difference.
The listeners wrote it, too.

PILOT
OF THE
AIRWAVES

Well here it is – a book about me! I've always refused
requests to do one. Who's interested?
I'm just a local lad on local radio doing the only thing
I'm good at – who owes it all to everyone else.
But Peter Grant and the Liverpool Echo were very
persuasive – threatening to do it with or without me!
So here it is – it's not an autobiography at all – it's just
a peep into where I came from, what makes me tick,
what makes me smile and hopefully what makes me what
I am. I hope it tickles a nostalgia gem and brings a smile.

Billy Butler

MRS BUTLER'S ELDEST

Introduction by Peter Grant

BILLY Butler has clocked up 50 years in showbiz – 40 of them as one of the nation's favourite disc jockeys.

From Cavern DJ to TV's Lucky Stars, singing in The Merseybeats and Tuxedos, presenting shows at Radio Merseyside then Radio City . . . then back to the Beeb.

Plus there's also THAT smash hit show Hold Your Plums.

He was honoured with tributes in his local papers and at the New Grafton Rooms where he was saluted by the Variety Club of Great Britain with A Tribute To Billy Butler.

At the time he said blushing, "I feel embarrassed – but very touched."

Billy's certainly touched with an ability to communicate with people from all walks of life . . . he doesn't take compliments easily. But he sure gives them out.

"I'm a great believer that in life if you get the chance to tell someone you love them you should do it before it's too late. It's great to be appreciated."

And he's got proof.

"One lady wrote to me for a dedication when her little baby was first born. Now that girl is a grown woman and I've played a dedication every year."

He loves such data and trivia titbits and, of course, he knows his audience.

He likes anything that's interesting . . .

It's one reason he has such a following.

"I know where to draw the line with others," he stresses.

Billy says his technique is simple – it's all down to doing things first then asking questions later.

"When I went to Radio Merseyside in the 70s I knew some people didn't want me there.

"But I knew my audience, I drank with them, I played the clubs with them. That audience is still with me."

Billy, who made a big impression on Radio 2, once turned down a Radio 1 job, but he has no regrets about any of his decisions. Except leaving the BBC in 1995 – he still says it was his biggest mistake.

Billy, of course has his critics – but as long as they listen to him that's OK.

"A young woman wrote to me saying that her mum always loved listening to my show and that she felt so close to us. Sadly, her mum died at 84 years of age – but the daughter told me that she looked forward to the programme every day it was on. She would sit there by the radio roaring with laughter. That's enough for me.

"Letters like that keep me going."

Some people to this day won't leave the house until it's been on. Others have been known to tape it while going to the shops. He also has a huge audience who listen on the web.

Billy Butler shows are committed (he should be) to giving a splendid time for all during the three hours it's on air.

As soon as the red light goes on he's away.

There's been bizarre slots: the singing telegram from Reliable Ronnie – a ventriloquists's dummy who called his boss Gilly Gutler.

There was Fascinating Sid, who brought in a list of "Did you know?" snippets, followed by a Caption Contest . . . on the radio.

One day it was a picture of the Queen's visit to The Kop. One caller rang in: "The Queen, dressed in ermine, sits down with her crown and robe and a Kopite behind her taps her on the shoulder and says: 'Ere, come straight from work, Queen?'"

The prizes varied. You could get a box at Goodison – it was actually a cardboard crate presented outside the ground. Or a signed Madonna photo – signed by Billy and Wally.

Then Billy would 'have a go' at something. VAT on

vegetables – MP's expenses . . . Ringo Starr.

"I know people at home are going, 'yeah you're right'"
he once told me.

Bill makes radio presenting seem easy. I have been on his
shows and forgotten I was on air.

So did his cleaning lady at the studio.

"Our cleaner Emma became a hit too," recalls Billy.

"We used to wind her up something rotten and she would
forget we were going out across Merseyside."

In this book of memories Billy first looks back at his own
life and then there's a collection of his classic musings in
the Liverpool ECHO called Remember When.

Timeless.

We raided his photo archive. We found out about his
favourite things in the Lists section – MBEs: My Best
Ever from Westerns to Beatles' songs.

And, oh boy, his knowledge of music, films, telly, you
name it he could go on Mastermind . . .

"Subject, Mr Butler?"

"EVERTHING."

Also in this literary radio show (beat you to it, Billy) we
turn the turn-tables on him.

He's made millions of dedications to other people so here
are dedications to HIM, a veritable Variety Club of Great
Britain . . . in print.

So welcome to the wonderful world of Billy Butler,
MBE.

Buy it now – don't wait till it ends up in a car boot sale.

FIVEWORDS

Why use one word when five will do?
It's never stopped Billy Butler.
Throughout his star-spangled life Billy has welcomed
many guests on his shows from all walks of life.
Now, here are some famous folk who wanted to say a few
kind words about Mrs Butler's Eldest.
First, all the way from Nashville – the Voice of Dr Hook.
And then a fab four of other household names.
So, to welcome you to this Billy Butler Show with a
difference, let the Fab Five introduce themselves,
to their great pal.

DENNIS LOCORRIERE
THE VOICE OF DR HOOK

I really wish I would have been awake that night 20 years ago when Billy called from the studio.

His intention, I'm sure, was to catch me off-guard and play a few games with me to the amusement of his listeners.

But I was asleep in my bed in Nashville, Tennessee.

Damn!

Billy got my answering machine and waited while I sang my outgoing message for all the world (and by that I mean Liverpool and the surrounding areas) to hear.

After the beep he shouted "POSER!" and let out that infectious, pornographic little laugh of his, slamming the phone down.

I talked to him a few days later and strongly objected to his chosen terminology.

"Poser?" I said. "You called ME! I was asleep!"

To this day I wish I would have been awake to take his call.

Because it would have been fun to talk to Billy.

It always is.

Whenever I'm on tour I try and manage to wangle my way onto his show for the express purpose of enduring as many of his well placed insults as I can.

The last time we spoke he mentioned seeing me at The Echo Arena with Bill Wyman's Rhythm Kings (what a kick for a child of the 60s like me to be in a band with a Rolling Stone!)

He said he learned something important about me while watching that performance.

That I can't dance!

I haven't actually counted them myself, but I've been told that Billy is celebrating 40 years as a broadcaster and 50 years in show business.

When I think of all the people from his illustrious past that might have been asked to write this forward I can't help but be very pleased with myself and extremely flattered.

By the way, Billy doesn't know I'm writing this bit yet, but I can hardly wait til he finds out and tells me how much he hates it.

It's sure to be a pisser!

LES DENNIS
TELEVISION PERSONALITY

Billy Butler is the voice of Liverpool. Whenever I travel back to the city by car I tune into Radio Merseyside as soon as I hit the M62. If I hear Billy's rich scouse tones I feel immediately at home. His style is intimate, funny and informative and all without effort.

People often ask me where we got the contestants for Family Fortunes. Quite clearly from the same place Billy got his for Hold Your Plums.

"Give us a clue Billy" became the city's catchphrase.

He asked a woman: "Which Hollywood actor had the nickname The Duke?"

She said "Give us a clue Billy" and he, doing his best John Wayne drawl replied, "The hell I will."

"Oh go on Billy," she cried "You give everyone else one". I nearly crashed into the car ahead.

Being interviewed by Billy is a treat. It's two mates reminiscing about Liverpool, its people, places and history.

Half an hour passes in a flash and he hasn't referred to his notes once. He is a walking archive. Everytime I go to his studio I leave with a DVD of a television show I don't even remember doing. He's got a copy of a deeply embarrassing single I recorded in the early 70s that he keeps threatening to play. Billy, please don't.

Liverpool is a richer and funnier place for having Billy Butler. Long may he reign.

JOE LONGTHORNE
ENTERTAINER

Billy has always been one of my greatest supporters and it is a very real pleasure to add my personal tribute. Without personalities such as Billy, his infectious laughter and great love of life, this world would be a far lesser place.

PETE BEST
FORMER BEATLE

I knew him as a schoolmate.
I knew him as a muso.
I knew him as a DJ.

I know him as a gentleman.

BILLY KINSLEY
MUSICIAN

I've known Billy since I was a kid. I lived on the opposite side of West Derby Road to Billy, or Bunna as he was affectionately known to his friends.

Like myself he was crazy about music even then and bought lots of records every week without fail. We realised we both loved rock 'n' roll, especially Buddy Holly, and we'd go to see all the latest British and American stars at the Empire Theatre.

When Eddie Cochran and Gene Vincent came over I couldn't afford a ticket and my brother and sister who usually took me there weren't going. Billy went on the first night – as it was on for four or five nights – and came home raving about how good the show was, asking me if I wanted to go. He got me a ticket and to this day I've never forgotten how kind he was to 'mug' me.

Billy was five or six years older than me and he still is (ouch!) but he accepted me into his circle of friends who were all mostly his age. With his vast knowledge of music he thought he was just what Thank Your Lucky Stars – the biggest pop show on television at the time – was looking for, to appear on the spin-a-disc panel which had members of the public guesting each week. Billy was so successful on his first appearance that the producer invited him, along with Janice Nichol and her "I'll give it five" in a strong

Brummie accent, back to be regular panellists. In those days it was strange to have a mate on the telly every week!

When we had the Merseybeats' Guest Night at St John's Hall in Bootle on Monday nights, Billy became our first guest and was advertised as 'The Mystery Guest Straight Off The Television'. He decided to come on stage with a hood on and sing the first song before he'd taken it off.

Most of the audience guessed who it was before he removed it. I've no idea how.

Billy joined us for a couple of months before leaving, mainly as a career move, to join The Tuxedos who came from the other end of West Derby Road. Lots of things have happened since then but Billy's brain is still working overtime, coming up with incredibly funny game shows like Hold Your Plums and I was delighted to be asked to write and record the theme song for that show.

However jealousy crept in one morning when I was listening to Billy and Wally when I couldn't believe my ears! They had Doris Day on their bloody show live!!!

Only he would have the guts to call Calamity Jane in California early on a Sunday morning and ask her on the show! I'd give anything for a recording of the conversation they had when she first picked up the phone and was asked by two mad Scousers to come on their show.

It's over 50 years since I first met Billy and I can't think of any other person who still gets so enthusiastic and passionate over music and records and he's not even a musician!

Long may he do so, and if you see him tell him I'll always be forever grateful for that trip to The Empire.

Thanks Bill.

MY MATE BILLY

by Wally Scott

BILLY and I first met in the 70s when he left Radio Merseyside to join Radio City.

I'd been asked to produce his new show and first impressions for both of us were not favourable. He thought I was 'a little upstart'.

And I decided he was a bit of a big 'ead. Fortunately those opinions soon changed and we not only became a successful broadcasting team, we also ended up great mates. So much so that in over 30 years we've never had a single fall out. Except perhaps over whose turn it was to get the ale in.

Not bad when we spent so much time living in each others pockets working on the radio six days a week while doing pantomimes, clubs, theatres and a weekly Channel One television show. Billy actually saw more of me than his attractive wife, Lesley. A bad swap.

Lots of people ask how the Billy and Wally partnership actually came about. Well, it was all down to Billy who started chatting to me on the air. At that time it was unheard of – the presenter talking to his producer.

Very soon, I was summoned to the office of Radio City's then MD, Terry Smith, who could be intimidating at the best of times. He told me in no uncertain fashion to cut out the on-air chat. I informed Billy who typically took not a blind bit of notice. I was again hauled up before Terry for another b******ing. But then the letters and phone calls started flooding in from listeners saying how much they enjoyed the banter between the two of us. Even Terry Smith was won over. He never raised the matter again.

Billy left City to rejoin Radio Merseyside and six months later I joined him there. It was here Billy dreamed up Hold Your Plums which was to become a cult programme with fans all over the world. Devotees creased up to callers like Margaret Hagan who was asked by Billy, which sporting object has 250 dimples on it.

My Mate Billy

The answer is, of course, a golf ball. But hapless Margaret blurted out: "Is it a sumo wrestler's arse, Billy?"

And there was Les Hollins from Wigan, who when asked where was Anne Boleyn beheaded, answered: "Was it just below the chin Billy?" The immortal words: "Give us a clue Billy" were born on the show.

Billy and I have laughed our way through the years. We used to do the yes-no interlude on the daily show where Billy would try to trick the caller into saying yes or no.

If they did I would gong them out. One time, at 2am in the morning, Billy rang me at home and said: "Is that you Wally?" Still half asleep I replied "yes" and he banged the gong at the other end of the phone.

Billy is a DIY sad case and we made a very funny feature of his disasters. Rapid Hardware even put up photos of Billy all over the shop accompanied by the words: "Don't serve this man!" He once put a mirror up in the bathroom while standing in the bath. Consequently the only way you could see in the mirror was to stand in the bath yourself.

And it was like something out of a Warner Bros cartoon when Billy stood perched with one foot on his garden wall and the other on a branch he was sawing off. He ended up crashing to the ground and being taken to hospital.

The Billy and Wally weekends at Pontins have been a huge success and are still going strong after over 50 such events. I remember one time coming back to my chalet at 1am in the morning to find the door boarded up. I had to call out the security to get in. I have a good idea I know who was involved. I also made the mistake of telling Billy I didn't eat red meat, only chicken. I arrived at my chalet one weekend to find it littered with over 200 chicken legs.

Guess who again. Yes, as I said before, me and Mrs Butler's Eldest have laughed a lot.

And we got paid for it. Can't be bad Billy lad.

BILLY THE KID

A cowboy childhood

AFTER I left school I went camping with the lads – it was the first time I'd ever been away from home on my own.

When you think about it these days – I was that far away from home, I was in Wales, I'd never been away from home on my own before and my mam didn't really know my mates.

There was no way of getting in touch, because we didn't have a phone at the time, so it must have been a hell of a strain on my mam, wondering where her little lad was.

I had a great time. We didn't get into trouble – we did do some things we shouldn't, but then what kids didn't?

Our street was a great street to live in.

We had the usual moaning neighbours, you know, because we played in the streets a lot – that's what we did in those days. There weren't as many cars so you could play in the street and there'd be a house one side as a goal and our house the other side as another goal and we played shots in, we played football, we played alallio, we played flinches, where you had to stand still and you threw the ball up in the air and you shouted the name of someone to catch it, and then you just stood still, and if they caught it they had to throw it at someone who was stood still, and I tell you what if you were close to someone and they threw it at you, they couldn't half get you.

I used to stand at one side of the street, throw a ball to the other side and make it hit the kerb and come back to you. We collected jinks from bottle tops – they were the tops from beer bottles and stuff like that, and we played games with jinks. We played nearest to the wall and we also made badges which ruined our sweaters 'cos if you took the cork bit out of the jink and put it on one side of your sweater, and the jink the other side and pressed the cork back into the jink, you had a jink badge.

The only snag is, when you took the jink off there was a great big lump in your sweater where the jumper had sucked out the material. They were great days – I really enjoyed my childhood.

We'd go to Newsham Park and go to the boating lake and try and catch fish. We played games, it was great. And like everybody's childhood it seemed to be summer all the time.

We didn't get a telly until I was about fourteen or fifteen, so I played out a lot actually. But when telly did come out I was fascinated by it and I did used to watch a lot though it took a lot to get me away from the radio because in the early days, when I was at the collegiate, the talking point was always Journey Into Space, one of the greatest radio shows ever, which filled your imagination to the brim.

Like everybody else in the sixties, I listened to Radio Luxembourg, because that was where all the new records were played. People forget that Radio Luxembourg had more than just music – they had Dan Dare Pilot of the Future, and they were the first to have Opportunity Knocks. They had Double Your Money, and Take Your Pick – lots of game shows. It was an incredibly interesting radio station and I'm just so sad that none of those early non-music based programmes seem to exist any more.

Oh, and there was Valentine Dyall – The Man In Black which I really remember as well. I used to love listening to the radio when I was a kid. I'd sit in the corner and my mam would be doing the ironing and I'd listen to Over The Garden Wall, and Take It From Here, and The Goons – it was fascinating.

My Grandad, who basically had taken the role of my dad once we moved into Grey Rock Street, persuaded me to join the Rankin Boys club. Before that, most of the sport I had was at the Collegiate, and of course every Saturday and Sunday we'd spend our time in Boaler Street school yard, climbing over the iron fence and playing football for about two hours each way.

It shows the respect we had for people in those days, because there'd be about twenty or thirty of us, and we'd pick teams, and I'd got reasonably good then so I used to be in the first four of five that we picked – I used to be the last to be picked but I'd improved a bit – and we'd play a couple of hours each way, and get a bottle of lemonade at half time and drink that ¬ but the respect we had for those in authority was funny. In fact I still remember the name of the caretaker – Mr Sutton. He used to come out suddenly and say "Come on you kids, out of the school yard." And believe it or not, all twenty of us would run and climb out and go. No turning on him or beating him or anything like that – respect for authority existed then.

So, my Grandad had got me to join the Rankin, and I had some great times there. I eventually made the first team and we won the League, we won the cup, we played at Goodison Park, we played at Anfield.

I had some fabulous times.

We had to go training, running around Newsham Park, if we were going to get picked for the football team.

Mr Jones, who was then in charge of the team, used to write a report after each game. I used to have some of them actually, until my Uncle Norman threw them out when we left Grey Rock Street. I missed those reports 'cos I got some good 'uns.

I remember there was one that said "Where have you been all the day my Billy Boy?" because I'd scored the winning goal for the Rankin, in my debut for them, against the top of the league. I'll never forget that. It was a fabulous boys' club and the LBA was a wonderful organisation.

At night time we basically used to hang around Boaler Street. I had a few mates from Boaler Street and a few from Grey Rock Street and we'd hang around corners talking about the latest films, latest TV series, and we weren't into drinking – not until we were sixteen or seventeen – because it was hard to get into a pub in those days. You had to memorise the year you were born, to make sure you were eighteen when you went in and the publicans were a lot stricter than they are now, so I didn't start any serious drinking until I was seventeen. Even then I only drank locally – to go to town, well, that was where all the old men went to drink as far as me and my mates were concerned. We weren't experienced enough to go into town and drink just yet.

Girls didn't really come along – I mean I went to the Grafton and the Locarno, but the difficulty was that I couldn't dance. It all started with this vixen of a woman, when I first ventured onto the dance floor, when there was a record playing, and as I walked towards the girl, her and her mate walked away, and the faster I walked towards them, the faster they walked away. And it was a knock-back that I never really recovered from.

So I hated dancing, to the extent that whenever we went to dance at the Locarno, and the lads would say "Are we getting up to dance, shall we split a couple of girls up – I always used to say I'd injured my foot playing football, and I'd bandage my foot so I wouldn't have to dance.

I don't know if they ever believed me, because I had a bandaged foot pretty regularly.

I loved going to the pictures – I've always loved the movies. And I was very lucky where we were because we could go to the Palladium, we could go to the Lido in Belmont Road, the Savoy in West Derby Road, the Hippodrome, the Litton in Everton Valley, the Cosy Lyton on Boaer Street, the Kensington – they were all within walking distance.

In those days, or course of a night, you couldn't get in unless you were with an adult, and it would probably frighten the life out of everyone these days to know that you used to say "Take one in, please," to a stranger, to get in. But that's the way it was in those days – we weren't told to be as frightened of strangers as we are now. So you'd stop someone and ask them to take you in.

I always remember one time that almost made me stop believing in God. I've never been a totally religious person but I used to say my prayers every night – selfish prayers that it wouldn't rain if we had football, or if Everton had an important game I'd pray that they'd win – but I'd still say God bless my Mam and my Grandad. I used to like going to Sunday school, I don't know whether they liked me 'cos me mates weren't the best behaved people in Sunday School. I remember when my mate Albert Myers was asked who led the Egyptians out of the desert and he said it was Charlton Heston. I think he believed it was actually.

Anyway, I was outside the Palladium and there was a movie on that I wanted to see – I think it was Quo Vadis. And I was saying "Take one in please?" and this man said, "Certainly, Son" and I put my money in his hand.

There was this other little kid who also said take one in, but the man said "I can't I'm already taking one in." And I said to the man "It's ok mister, I'll wait for the next one, take him in." And he said "That's very kind of you, son" and he gave me my money back and took him in.

And honest to God, I thought to myself "Well that was a nice thing I did, God'll remember that." And after five minutes I said to somebody else "Take one in please," and he said "Certainly, son," and I thought "Well there we are, that's been noticed." But when we got to the cash box, the woman said "Sorry, it's full," and I walked away thinking "Well thanks very much God."

It almost shook my faith in religion.

My first job was at Perrin Hughes – a plumbers' merchants – working behind the counter selling toilets and stuff like that. And it was while I was there that I got the job on Thank Your Lucky Stars. It was funny because I got that job after going for an audition in Manchester. We had to sit there and talk about records we'd heard. And then I heard nothing at all, and the show had started, and I used to watch it each week and I'd say "I remember him at the audition, I was as good as him, they could have picked me."

Out of the blue I got this letter asking me to go along to Birmingham and record the show.

I was obviously over the moon being on television. And when we did it the producer, Philip Jones, said "That was very good, that's the best panel we've had, would you like to come on again?" And I said "Yeah, I'd love that."

So two weeks later, I got another letter asking me to go and record the show in Birmingham, which I did, and over the next year I was on it 20 or so times, including the two all-Liverpool specials.

But the funny thing was, nobody approached me to do anything else, there were no agents in touch with me. And when you bear in mind that I was a little lad from Liverpool of 19 or 20, on national television every Saturday, not even the Echo put anything in. The only person who did put anything in was George Harrison in Over the Mersey Wall, and there was a picture of Helen Shapiro in it, and it said "Who was the cheeky Scouser who appears each week on Thank Your Lucky Stars? It's Billy Butler of 52 Grey Rock Street."

And that was it, but it was great for me, walking around town, with people looking at me saying "Aren't you that fella off the television?"

It did help me pull, of course, that's a very important part of it. But nothing really happened until I was asked to join a group, The Cherry Pickers, I think it was, and we then changed our name to The Hangmen.

We used to play at the pub opposite the stadium and we

played at The Odva, in Bootle, and then two lads, Les Williams and Alan Crowley, who were mates of mine from Bowler Street and Kensington, joined the group, and eventually that evolved into The Tuxedos. But before that, because I had been on telly, I'd been asked by The Merseybeats to be their guest star, and I did the Bootle Town Hall, as a masked celebrity. And I've still got the Bootle paper where it says "Masked man storms it at the Town Hall" and there are picture of all the girls screaming at me while I'm on stage. Great experience, that.

I did about half a dozen gigs with The Merseybeats at the Cavern and places like that. I met The Beatles a couple of times, and drank with them over at the White Star and The Grapes, and they kept asking me questions like, what were the people on Lucky Stars like?

I never thought of myself as anything special, as a celebrity or anything like that, as they do these days. I just took it as part of life's game, part of the way things happen.

Basically though, that was the stepping stone, because after The Tuxedos I played football for the Merseybeat Eleven, and I commentated on the second half at one of the games, and from that Bob Wooler asked me if I'd like to DJ at the Cavern, and I said, yes, I'd give it a go, and I did, and that was it from then on. I started as a Cavern DJ and that was my first step on the ladder.

CAVERN DAYS

Billy Butler, the DJ

I HAD some good days with the band.

Basically, the band started up because I used to go to town in the early sixties, and visit the clubs where they were playing music.

There were hardly any late night clubs in Liverpool at the time, and I remember going to an all night session at the Iron Door, and I got up to sing with Steve Bennett and The Syndicate because he had asked if there was anyone in the audience who knew the words to What Did I Say. Then I was approached by a group called The Hangmen, and I sang with them for a while – we mainly played the pub opposite the Stadium called the Cross Keys and we used to get changed in the toilets downstairs.

Then we became The Cherry Pickers, and Alan and Johns and John from The Tuxedos joined, and we changed our name to Billy Butler and The Tuxedos.

We didn't do much, but we had some laughs. We had quite a lot of bookings – we worked out of town once in Stoke. We were very big at Hope Hall actually, because we weren't the best of groups, and we started sending ourselves up there, and they loved it, so we became very popular at Hope Hall.

We played The Cavern quite a few times, I remember one time when The Beatles had just made it big and were touring and everybody was throwing jelly babies at them.

So when we did The Cavern I thought "This is a good idea, I'll throw jelly babies at the crowd." So I threw jelly babies and they threw sandwiches, pieces of paper, anything they could find on the floor, all back at us.

Then, of course, I was DJ-ing at a football match when Bob Wooler asked me to DJ at The Cavern. I had some great times there. I met some fabulous people and appeared with some legendary groups. I considered myself very, very lucky. And if I had known how popular The Cavern was going to be I'd have enjoyed it even more.

When The Cavern shut down I worked all over the place – The Downbeat, The Mardi Gras, and The Parr Hall in Warrington, I worked in a pub called The Last Inn, and I worked in Oswestry. I played mostly soul music, so I kept myself going until The Cavern re-opened. I worked in Wigan, at the Paradise Club, the Las Vegas, and The Queens – lovely people in Wigan.

The big change came when I was working at The Mardi Gras doing the soul nights with my business partner, Chris Wharton, and we were offered the chance to take over at the club, which we did. We continued with the soul music but unfortunately we had a lot of trouble and had to abandon it, and use instead what was called progressive groups.

We had people like Uriah Heap, The Pink Fairies, Status Quo, Argent – a lot of really great progressive bands, and we were the only ones doing it and we were doing really, really well. And then we got a Close Down Order and that was that. We did have a look at the Hippodrome, with the Whitbreads brewery, who were very good to us, and we were going to turn that into a rock venue, and that would have been absolutely brilliant, but it didn't happen, and I can't complain.

I don't remember much about my dad, because my dad left my Mam and he only came back occasionally. And every time he did come back it seemed that my Mam was pregnant.

We lived in Phoebe Anne Street till I was about five, and then we went to live with my grandparents. I don't remember much about Phoebe Anne Street except that my Uncle Paddy and Aunty Dot used to live there. Later on they moved to Dovecot, and when I was living in Grey Rock Street I used to go up there on the 75 bus every second weekend, because they used to keep the Film Fun for me.

I couldn't wait to get there to read it. Grey Rock Street was a great street to live in – we had great neighbours who all knew each other. If anybody ever passed away there was always a collection that went around the streets to take money for them, and all the houses either side of the street drew their curtains. Mums used to play out in the street with their children – my Mam used to play rounders with us.

In fact I remember a day when she was playing with us and somebody threw the ball to her and she really smacked it. She was really strong, my Mam, probably because she used to wash all of our clothes by hand, and she had muscles that she used to say to us "Have a look at that muscle." She used to smack us and I don't disrespect her for that. She only ever smacked us if we were naughty, she never smacked us for nothing, and sometimes she'd say to me "God sent you down here to punish me," or "You're just like your father, you are," which I could never understand because I couldn't remember anything about him.

Anyway, back to the rounders – we threw the ball to my Mam and she hit it and it went right threw a neighbour's window. And I turned to my Mam to say, look what you've done, and she was gone. She'd raced straight into the house and shut the door. The neighbour came out, and because I had the bat in my hand, they assumed it was me, took me to our house, knocked on our door and said "Mrs. Butler, your Billy has just broken our window."

And Mam said "I'm awfully sorry Mrs Hignett, I'll make sure he pays for it. Now get in you." And she dragged me in. And it wasn't me at all, but my Mam felt too embarrassed to say it was her.

It was a great street to play in. It was a big street and it had a top, a middle, and a bottom. And we knew everybody in the middle, quite a few at the bottom, and a few at the top, so even though the streets were big, the neighbours were very close.

I got married in 1963 I think it was, and I got divorced in 1984. I had two good lads – Stuart and Lee. Our Lee's done very well for himself, whether it's in the genes or not I don't know, but he was recently voted the club DJ of the year. He's a dance DJ, he's not like me – I'm a talking DJ – he does all the mixing and he's got skills that I never had.

In fact that's one of the reasons I packed it in. I DJ'd around all the clubs until 1984, and I had my last residency at Clouds in Litherland. I used to do Thursday, Friday and Saturday there until one o clock in the morning.

And it started happening that the mixing came in so records were coming out as so many beats per minute and you could time them so one record flowed into the next.

Now I'm not the most skilful of operators so when that came in I decided that ok, I'd had a good run, I'd been DJ-ing around the clubs for over 20 years, I've got the radio so I'll give the club game a miss.

But then something came from that because I'd moved to Radio City in 1978, and got together with Wally Scott, and we started putting the Billy and Wally shows on. And that's still going on now and even though lots of clubs are closing down, we still sell out at the Brindley, the Gladstone, the Civic in Ellesmere Port and St Helens Theatre. People always say we provide the right variety at the right price.

I also had great pleasure doing Radio Merseyside's annual birthday shows at the Empire, and I'm very pleased to say that we sold out every show we've done. The last one was called 40 Years of Music and Laughter and we featured musical acts and comedy acts from across the Merseyside broadcast area. There's so much talent in Liverpool, and on Radio Merseyside.

I'm pleased to say, we broke our records as well.

Jennifer Rush's Power Of Love – I've got a gold disc

from CBS congratulating me on helping to break that. We broke Mississippi by Pussycat, and we were the only radio station in the UK to break Wuthering Heights by Kate Bush, as our record of the week.

So the radio station itself has got a great track record in spotting hits. And, of course, we've always supported local bands – as I've always said if you can't ask a local station for help who can you ask?

I've always been a big fan of the movies, and I've already said we had lots of picture houses round by where we lived. It was just a Saturday afternoon and maybe one or two nights in the week. We used to take lemonade bottles back and run messages to try and get money to go to the pictures. And when it rained – I know people say summer was always sunny but you always think that about when you were a kid – that's where we were.

I met Les and we got married in 1990. So we've been married 20 years.

We've got two boys – Paul and David and David himself has been DJing at a club in Birkenhead.

And once again, as with our Lee, it wasn't with any encouragement from me, it was just something that he wanted to do.

Mind you, we're living in an age now where a lot of kids want decks for presents – they see themselves as being the club DJ's of the future. And of course lots and lots of clubs in town are dance clubs and so there are opportunities, although it's not something you can base your whole career on. I mean I was DJ-ing at The Cavern, working during the day and doing the radio as well.

So you can't just rely on the one thing, you've got to have a couple of eggs in your basket – just in case one of them is cracked and falls apart.

But meeting Les was great because she encourages me – she supports me and gives me ideas – she's a ball of fun herself and even though there's a 20-year age difference, I think it's helped me stay young in my thinking, which on radio, of course, is an asset.

The thing about the radio show is that I've always tried to get out and meet people – I think that's very important.

Early on in my days in radio, when I started in 1971, by 1972/3 I was organising Billy Butler Get Togethers in which I'd get a club in town – for nothing if we filled it – we used to do the Shakespeare a lot actually, and I'd tell my listeners to come along and meet me. I'd get a couple of local acts in, who we'd been playing on the radio, to entertain them and we used to fill the place, two or three times a year, and it was a great way of getting to know all the people who are listening to you.

They'd tell you what they thought of the show and whether you were doing right or wrong.

I've always been a great believer in having the right record to suit the occasion so if there's a loss in the family, or a break-up, or a birthday or celebration I always have a record to suit that event. I don't believe in reading a request out for something personal and then just playing a record that has nothing to do with the occasion.

People often ask me how I do it, but, as I tell them, IT'S MY JOB. If I was a plumber or an electrician I'd have to know what I was doing. I always like having a bit of fun on the radio. We were the first to do gargling on the radio, in fact, I think I was the first to bring the producer into the radio show.

When I started at Radio City in 1978, and I'd bring Wally Scott into the show, he used to get told off afterwards upstairs. The bosses used to tell me "Don't be calling your producer in – you're presenting the show." But I knew it worked, and we've more than proved that since. Because I'd collected records for years, by people who were only singing just because they were famous, we started a thing called "Bet You Don't Know Who This Is" – which were songs by people who weren't really singers. And that's been picked up by many others in different ways.

I started a show on City on Sunday afternoon called Heads and Tails, in which people got a question right, and we tossed the coins and they had to guess whether it was going to come down heads or tails.

And there's a story behind that because when I went to Radio Merseyside again in 1983, Head and Tails was already very successful for Radio City so they handed it over to Norman Thomas. So I had to come up with another idea for Radio Merseyside to compete with my own idea at Radio City and that's how I came up with Hold Your Plums.

And I always remember going to see Ian Judson, who was boss at the time, God bless him, and I've been lucky in this game in having some bosses who really went along with what I was trying to do, and I gave him my new idea for the show. I said: "It's like a fruit machine – you answer a question and you pull the arm and if you get three bells or three cherries you win a prize."

"Great idea m'lad," he said, "and what are you going to call it?" I said "Hold Your Plums."

He said: "What? I don't know about that bonny lad, can't you call it Hold Your Bells?" I said "No, that's why I want to call it Hold Your Plums."

So he said: "I tell you what, I'll send it to the Radio Times for the programme listings and if they print it we're in." And they printed it, and that's how Ian Judson played one of the big parts in Hold Your Plums coming about.

Wally and I also did a show called Take Your Chicks, in which listeners came on the line, and answered a question which entitled them to win a part of a chicken.

They'd win a leg or a breast, or a wing until they had a complete chicken, and then they'd go for the whole chicken and could Take Your Chick. We did Hide and Seek on air where two callers were on the line and one caller would go and hide somewhere in their house, and give the phone to someone else in the house and the other contestant would ask questions and try and guess where the person was hiding. We had one lady who was on for two weeks and we found out that she was hiding in a shelter at the bottom of the garden. We also had Strip on air, where people came on the line and if they got the question wrong they had to take something off.

And they had to tell us on air exactly what it was they were taking off.

We've played Pontoon on air, and we've adjusted Hang Man to suit the radio. And that's what radio's all about — coming up with new ideas all the time to keep yourself fresh and on top.

PLUM JOBS

Laughter and tears

I FIRST met Wally when I joined Radio City in 1978. And funnily enough, before that I didn't really like him because I used to see him in the New Court Bar, which was next to Radio Merseyside in Sir Thomas Street, and he used to be sitting on a stool posing, as far as I was concerned, with his shirt open right down to his waist, and stuff like that, and I always thought to myself "Poser!"

Anyway he ended up as my producer.

I created this image for Wally of being a desperate bachelor, in search of any woman at all as long as she wore suspenders. He played up to it.

From then on we started doing cabaret and stuff like that and we created a really good thing together. I invented the game shows and it was great – plain sailing. But when I decided to return to Radio Merseyside, it was on my own.

Ian Judson approached me and asked me if I'd like to come back. I wasn't totally unhappy at Radio City but Ian made a very persuasive case, and I gave my notice in at Radio City and moved over to Merseyside.

I was about a year at Merseyside before I had a chat with Wally – I bumped into him and asked him would he care to come over, and he was rather unhappy the way things were going at City although, give him his due, because he's a good producer he'd made a good job with my replacement Johnny Kennedy.

So Wally came back over in 1984, I think it was. I'd already come up with the idea for Hold Your Plums, and we started doing that show and it became an absolute legend.

Wally and I still work together.

When we went back to Radio City in 1995, he just became totally disillusioned with people who'd hardly been in radio telling him what to do and how to produce, and in the end he just threw his cards in and said: "No, I'd rather not be doing it, than be told what to do by people who've not been in the business five minutes."

So, we split up then and I continued at Radio City until 2000 when I started back at Radio Merseyside.

We still work together doing Pontin's. We've just completed more than 50 Pontin's gigs – and we've sold out every single one.

We do the theatres together and we've proved that if you put a variety show on with the right cast at the right price people will come and see you.

Wally's worked a bit himself since, on the radio – he's done Dune radio and a bit for a satellite station and he's still got more ideas than most of the producers that are in radio today.

It's a waste that he's not still working in radio.

I find, when you're growing up as a kid you have mates and mates are really important, obviously. They're the ones you call for, to play out.

I think in my early years, up to when I went to the Collegiate, and after, my mates were Bobby and Albert.

Bobby Thomas lived in the top end of our street, I lived in the middle, and we were mates. We played out together, we went to the pictures together, we ran messages together, and we got in trouble together.

When I started drinking my main pal was a lad called Lenny Fahey – no longer with us. He was a good mate of mine – I'd known him for a few years because when I started at the Collegiate and mixed with different people I mixed with a gang from Molyneaux Road and we used to hang out on the corner, talking about the latest records and stuff like that.

There was David Wilson and his brother, Freddy and Billy Green, Lolly Morris, Geoff Tobin and lots more, in fact they're the gang I first went camping with Llangollen.

We went back there camping a few times and I remember

being in Llangollen when Eddie Cochran was killed in a car crash.

We used to climb up this really high mountain – as we thought it was – and descend into a valley and there was a little canyon and we used to camp there.

There was a stream there and there was wood to collect, and we'd walk into Llangollen along the canal – why spend money on bus fare if you can walk it? We used to sit in a little café just near where you went up to book a canoe – it's a furriers or taxidermist now.

We used to sit there all day and play the juke box. It was threepence a go or five for a shilling and we'd listen to all the new records. They were wonderful times they really were.

They were really strict in Llangollen – we were only fifteen anyway – and it was very difficult to go into a pub and get a drink in those days. They'd want to know your age and if you didn't look your age they wouldn't serve you.

We had some fabulous times there and the few photographs that I've got of when we were camping bring back so many happy memories of the first time in my life that I was all on my own, with my mates, not getting told when to come in or go to bed, and they were brilliant days.

I went to a 60th birthday – I think it was Freddy Green's – and I met the Tobins and Geoff Leech and it was brilliant seeing them all again.

When I first got married I lived with my first wife's parents in Huyton, and by then I'd already started working in the day and working at the Cavern – and it gave me enough to get my first house which was a little place off Boaler Street – where I'd grown up – in Cambria Street.

After I'd been on the radio, still working at night in the clubs – and got more successful I managed to buy a house in Crosby.

When we got divorced I lost that house and most other things, and shortly after that I met Lesley and we decided to buy a house in Wallasey. Really, with the divorce settlement, I didn't have much left and it was the only area where I could afford to get a place big enough to house my collection – the ones in Liverpool of that size were far too expensive.

So I moved over to Wallasey and I've lived there ever since.

But of course I work in Liverpool and I've still got lots of friends there. It's funny in radio because when you mention anything people always catch up on it and I've never made any secret of the fact that I was born in Anglesey – in Salem Street – and was only there for six months.

We were evacuated there – it's funny that I still get mail telling me I should go back to Wales and that I'm not a real Scouser. But who cares what some people think?

I know I am a Scouser.

One of the most difficult, but also proudest moments of my broadcast career, was during the Hillsborough disaster.

I stayed on the radio right throughout the disaster, over the weeks following, and I'm very proud of the way I conducted the programme during that time. It was a time of great mourning and great loss on Merseyside and I think on my morning programme I managed to sympathize with the people listening and also give them a lot of comfort. That was when my knowledge of music really came to the fore because we'd do phone-ins and talk to people who had been affected by the tragedy. We had live discussions over who was to blame, and I remember The Sun reporter coming in to the studio to take a picture and I chased him.

He basically ran out of the studio in Paradise Street with me after him.

It was a very, very difficult period but my knowledge of

music enabled me to pick the right songs to comfort people who were listening, and those who were in need of some kind of belief or solace. I received a large amount of mail after Hillsborough and I've kept all of it because I'm very proud of the way I conducted the programme at that time.

I've done alright on television as well, since my first break on Thank Your Lucky Stars.

There were big gaps from then until the Mersey Pirate in the late seventies.

I was asked to audition and I passed, and the Mersey Pirate came out live from the Royal Iris.

It was presented by Dougie Brown – I was the entertainments officer and it was my role to provide entertainment on the boat. But also on the boat were two stowaways – Scully and Mooey – played by Drew Schofield and Ray Kinsley, which was the first television had seen of Scully and Mooey, who would later get their own brilliant series.

My job mostly featured looking for them on the boat and it was hysterical working with them. They were both a pair of scallywags in real life as well and we had some laughs with them.

After that, television work came thick and fast.

I presented Granada's What's On for quite a while, I had quite a few slots on Live from Two, which was an afternoon programme. I was featured on that clog dancing, and wrestling, as well as going around museums and different places doing many, many various things.

I also tested for a job on the Fun Factory which came live from a warehouse in Manchester of a Saturday morning – it took over from Tiswas and that was a terrible thing to try and do because Tiswas was absolutely unique and brilliant – we did our best for sixteen weeks. I actually tested for the role, again, of entertainment officer, but they couldn't find a presenter and suddenly they asked if I'd like to have a go at presenting. So I did, and I fronted the Fun Factory for sixteen weeks which was also the first taste of television for Jeremy Beadle.

It proved to me that in television you depend a lot on your producer and director. If you come up with ideas, and the producer and director think "Yeah, we can do that," sometimes it can come off.

I remember on the Mersey Pirate I came up with an idea to get a famous person to walk the plank. We were going to ask the kids to write in and tell us who they'd like to see walk the plank. Then we count the votes at the end of the week and do a cartoon of that famous person with their face on, and a sword pricking them to make them walk the plank and fall into the water. Unfortunately, the producer said no as the person who was chosen that week might get offended, and so we didn't do it.

I also remember way, way back, suggesting to Granada that film trivia was still great, but TV trivia was what was growing. This was in the very early 80s and I suggested a programme that had a panel that watched clips of old TV, but no, they didn't think that was a good idea. And yet after that there was show after show of panelists trying to guess famous television series and themes, but that's the way it goes.

I also presented a chat show called A Wacker's World and each of the weeks was based on a different theme like entertainment, business, first chance, things like that and that was very good – I interviewed some great people on that show, like Count Bartelli, the wrestler, Tom Williams from Liverpool Football Club, Rex Makin, Derek Hatton – that was very successful.

Then I presented a show called What The Butler Sees, which was where I went out and about talking to people and that went very well. I still do the occasional appearance on television whenever it comes up because

I've always enjoyed it. I think a lot of my success has come from the fact that I've never been anybody other than myself.

When I came on to local radio in 1971 – I think I'd had the right kind of upbringing, going through the rock and roll era, I'd gone through Merseybeat.

I'd only been a lad working for a plumber's merchants and it's funny you know the way things are in life.

I'm not an angel – when we were camping in Wales we once broke into a little shed – there was a hole in it and it said if you like the view put a donation in – and we climbed in through the window and we were going to take the money out of the box – it was in Betws-y-coed I think – and I'm in there and next minute I hear: "What are you doing there?" and there's a man standing at the window.

What happened to my mates? I don't know but there was just a cloud of dust going down the hill and I was arrested, with a mate, and put into a jail in Betws-y-coed, and it was harrowing for my Mam because she'd not brought me up that way.

I had to go to court a few months later and I was given a conditional discharge. And I also had another brush with the law when I was working down the docks. I was coming out of the docks and a policeman called me over and said: "What have you got?" I said "Nothing." I had to empty my pockets and I had a wagon wheel.

He said "Where did you get that?" and I said "It's my carrying out." And he looked at it and said "You've come a long way – these came from America." And, believe it or not, he arrested me, took me down to Strand Road Police station. The police then came and searched my house – did they think I was a secret hoarder of Wagon Wheels? They searched my house and I had to go to court and I was found guilty of that and fined a couple of pound, I think it was.

But I learned my lesson and that was that and I've been a law abiding citizen since.

THOSE WERE THE DAYS

Billy the blue nose

THE TWIST

FUNNILY enough I've never really been confident with girls – it all dates back to those days at the Grafton, that I mentioned before.

That was so embarrassing and completely shattered my confidence. I think the only time I really did get any confidence was when the Twist came in, because I could Twist.

And I've always been very wary of approaching girls because of the fear of rejection – which did happen, I must admit, on many, many occasions.

It's a wonder I never went into a monastery really, I got knocked back so many times.

And another funny thing – I've never ever had a manager.

I've always knocked on doors and luckily they've opened, but I've never actually had a manager.

I've just seemed to get through life and get the jobs myself.

Doors opened, and I went through them and there was something waiting for me on the other side.

It was only in the mid-eighties that I actually got an agent, and that was Tommy and Lyn from Power Promotions, and they're still my agents now.

I hope they will be for a long time because they are two really, really nice people, and they really know their job.

Lyn's gone on to become possibly the Best Events Manager that the Variety Club North West have ever had, and presently she has just taken over the Liverpool Branch, because they have all been amalgamated into one big North Western Branch.

So, hopefully, now that Lyn's back, something will be happening with the Liverpool Branch, which hasn't really done much over the years.

CHANNEL ONE

Going around with the Billy Butler Show with Wally, has been absolutely brilliant because we've used so many local acts. Going back to television, I forgot to mention our Channel One programme. When Channel One started – the first cable television network in Liverpool – I was approached to do a variety show, live from the Atlantic.

We had a very, very small budget – just the two cameras.

We recorded it of a Wednesday night at the Atlantic pub down the dock road using all local acts and it was incredibly successful. We were the most watched cable television show in the area, which we were delighted with because Wally and I scripted the whole thing.

Power Promotions booked the acts, who gave their services free for the TV exposure, and it worked really well.

We carried on then to doing it from Dino's off Kensington, and then from there Dicky Lewis's in the city centre and it was very, very successful. Looking back, we did about 50 or 60 of them, and we must have used over 200 local acts. I've still got copies of most of them, and looking back at them, they really do stand up.

It's great to see some of the people, who were on those early shows, who have made it really big since then.

We've had some funny experiences as well.

We once had Doctor Hook on – or rather Ray, who's the one with the patch not the one who's written the foreword in this book – and when he'd finished with the show he went next door to the Iron Horse, which was a Country and Western pub – and had a few to drink and got up on stage.

I always remember the barman telling me that one of the guys at the bar said: "Look at the state of him, he thinks he's Doctor Hook." Little did he know – he was!

But that was very successful – Billy and Wally's Big Night Out, and it still stands the test of time today.

EVERTON

I had some great times as the Everton Announcer as well.

I've always been an Everton supporter. I started going to games to watch Everton when I was probably 10 or 11 – as soon as I could afford the nine pence to go in the boy's pen.

And like everybody did in those days, we never got a bus.

If it was in walking distance we walked there. Because that saves money for bus fare – it was the same when I went to the Collegiate – I walked so that I would have some money to spend in the tuck shop. Well it was the same for the football match, as it was when we used to go to New Brighton Tower.

I used to go there a lot to watch the big rock and roll bands. They used to have some incredible shows there with the Beatles and Jerry Lewis, and Manfred Mann, and many more. The Rolling Stones were there as well. We'd get the ferry to Seacombe, and we'd walk the rest of the way to New Brighton, because it was cheaper to do that than to get the boat to New Brighton, and every penny counted when there were slot machines about.

So we would walk to the match, and we'd discuss the previous week's results on the way, because don't forget, I'm talking about days when there was no football on telly, and the only way you could see pictures of goals and pictures of the famous stars, was in the Saturday edition of the Liverpool Echo, or in the Sunday papers, or in the Daily Post.

In those days, six out of ten kids used to keep a scrap book and they cut out all the football pictures from the Sundays and the weeklies, and they'd stick them in it.

And unlike now, when there are football magazines galore, there was only one football magazine and that was the Charlie Buchan Monthly, and that was the only place where you could read about your favourite player and find out what he did.

You could even send away for postcard pictures of your famous footballer.

I've always wondered, you know, in those early days of football, whether or not the players themselves ever got any money from the people who put out those picture post cards. I bet they didn't – and that's a change from today.

In fact the first time I ever cried over a football match – was in the early 50s listening to the radio in Mrs Hatch's, who used to live in number 79 Grey Rock Street.

Everton got beat 4-3 in the FA Cup semi-final.

I remember that because I used to mind her house for her and she used to slip me threepence, and there was a man who used to come there who I called Uncle Jimmy.

He used to bring along one of those big boxes of Maltezers, and to a kid like me they used to look gigantic and they looked like there was hundreds and hundreds of Maltezers. And the first girl I ever fell in love with lived there as well – Marjorie Hatch.

I was nine or 10 I think, and she was about 16, and me and Albert Myers fell in love with her. We used to have rows about her and so we agreed that we would have half each. Tragically, Marjorie died of Leukaemia when she was only 17, but she was a lovely girl and she was very kind to me and it was a great shock and a great loss obviously.

In our house, there was me, my Mam, me Grandad who I called father, and my Grandma, who was Ginny.

My brother Stephen and sisters, Dot, Eilleen and Joan all in a three up and three down. My memories of Ginny sitting in the corner by the fire with a bowl on her legs full of cuins (or winkles) and she'd stick this pin in and pull this wriggly little thing out and put it in her mouth – ooh I hated it. And she used to eat tomatoes with sugar on as well. I always felt guilty over my grandma because when you're kids you're not at your most obedient and sometimes she'd have to chase us to bed, and sometimes she'd have to come up to tell us to be quiet. Mam hardly ever went out, once my dad had left us, because my grandad always said that it wasn't right for her to be seen going out.

In fact it was funny because me Mam was a grown woman with five kids but my grandad hated her smoking so she had to pretend she'd given it up. And many's the time my Mam would be upstairs sitting by the fireplace and she'd be blowing smoke up the chimney so my grandad wouldn't know that she smoked.

I've always tried to be as honest as possible on the radio, and what annoys me most about life is when you get the big companies doing something which you know is wrong, and you know that something should be done about it, but you can't, and you fell helpless. You get the big companies putting up prices and they never go down again. You have prices varying from one place to another.

You get people getting beat up and the people who do it get let off with stupid sentences, and I always let myself go on the radio about this kind of thing. And the nice thing is when people write in and say "Billy, you've said exactly what I was thinking. Thank goodness somebody will say what ordinary people are thinking."

I think that's about it really because I'm just the same as everyone else, injustice really annoys me.

Bullying really annoys me, as does people thinking you're stupid and then who then try to con you, and the fact that I'm on air and I can speak out about it on the radio I think gives listeners satisfaction because I'm saying what they think.

I think that has really helped me in my radio career.

I'm really proud of the fact, that not only did we used to celebrate every birthday that Radio Merseyside had with sell out shows at the Empire, with a line-up that I formulated, but also in the mid to late eighties and early nineties Radio Merseyside even promoted their own summer season at the Floral Pavilion in New Brighton and used to do every Friday and Saturday for eight weeks in the summer.

We did that for a couple of years and again we sold every one of them out. In fact Radio Merseyside probably did more shows at the Floral Pavilion in those days than anyone, because it was supporting your local theatre.

We used to do the Empire quite a lot and if there were any big rock and roll stars over, we'd put them on the Empire.

And we would always make sure that the supporting bill was local acts, because obviously it's everyone's ambition to appear at the Liverpool Empire. And if we couldn't get a big name, we'd fill the bill with local acts.

They always worked.

It's musical knowledge, knowing what your audience like, what the taste of the area is, and I got frustrated by the fact that at Radio Merseyside we'd be playing some records and people would phone up and ask where they could buy that record.

I'd say to go to their record shop and they'd tell me that they had and the shop didn't know it, or they can't order it because it's not in the Top 40. Explain this – how can a record get in the Top 40 if you don't order it?

So how can you say, "It's not in the Top 40, we haven't got it"? So I decided, in the late eighties, to see if I could license these songs.

So I got in touch with the record companies, and based on what I had been playing throughout the year – a mixture of records that were out then but the record shops couldn't be bothered ordering and oldies I played which I'd made into firm favourites.

With a combination of the two, I put together a cassette

called The Hits You Couldn't Get – it was an LP and cassette, and it was the biggest seller on Merseyside – it out sold everything.

It was so successful we had volumes two, three and four.

All of them were incredibly successful. That's knowing your area and knowing your music. There was a singer called Jimmy Rosselli who Radio Merseyside got behind, from America, and we played him a lot which made him a big name in the area.

He brought out a double cassette, which the record shops didn't seem to be bothering with, so we ordered a couple of thousand and sold every single one of them. In other words, know what the public want and give it to them and you can't go far wrong.

Those were the days.

REMEMBER WHEN...

On my radio shows, looking back on life plays a great part. I've always said nostalgia isn't what it used to be. But it is – it never changes. I just asked listeners to . . . "Remember when" – whether it was school days, the rag and bone man or first dates.

So join me now for a trip down memory lane . . . again.

SCHOOL DAYS

Your schooldays are the happiest days of your life – although you don't realise that until years afterwards.

The fun you had – especially in the playground – when you think of it now, there used to be classes of 50.

You can imagine what the playing area was like. It must have been like coming home from the footy match, there were that many bodies. How we managed to play football and cricket with that many people continually running across our path, well, I've still no idea.

If I try to think (and shudder) back to my old school reports, I'm almost certain they said I was 'disruptive' and 'talked too much in class.'

I was always the ringleader in something that went around the school like wildfire such as 'who could sneeze the loudest'. I'd start off with a pretend sneeze, and then someone would follow me with one that was louder. But the only trouble was sometimes you'd be too realistic and you'd end up with two streams running down your face.

Another thing sticks in my mind when I think about back to those days, going back to the playground was something that must have seemed like a modern miracle.

There were all those games going on – about ten football matches at once and all these kids charging around and the whistle would sound and everything would just STOP – immediately!

I was at Whitefield Road Primary School. It had two playgrounds – one for the boys and one for the girls. We used to often go into the girls' playground to skit them, because we'd be playing all these great games and they'd be skipping!

There were only ever two kinds of caretaker. The Gestapo-type or the really dead kind ones – there was never any in-between. But the dread in my school was getting sent out of class.

Our headmaster had the name to end all names for head teachers – Mr Caine.

He'd always be walking up and down the corridors and he was a disciplinarian, God bless him.

If you got sent out of the classroom, you'd stand there in total fear of Mr Caine walking down the corridor.

He'd ask: "What have you been sent out for boy?"

You'd tell him and he would then cane you. When he caned you, he left a mark right across your hand. One fella in our class was always misbehaving and getting into trouble. He'd get sent to Mr Caine and, when he came back, the teacher would always say: "Let me see your hand."

But this lad was clever. He would run up and down this staircase, which had a very narrow steel balustrade round it, to get a line on his hand. One day he got sent to the head and was gone for ages. He had run up and down the stairs, to get the mark on his hand, tripped, and broken his leg!

Then there was the school visits you'd look forward to – or not look forward to?

One of the regulars at our school was the police coming to put a puppet show on, which was somehow supposed to demonstrate road safety. But the visit you really dreaded was that made by the nit-nurse.

She'd be at the front of the class and you'd go to her one by one in front of everyone else.

And how did we survive those fights in the school playground? I'd get home with the kind of bumps you see in cartoons. You always knew there was a fight because you'd hear all the lads chanting: "Ooo! Ooo!" But no one ever fought. People just bumped each other's shoulders, fell on the ground together and then got it stopped.

Also on the playground, all the mums of the well-off kids used to come down at play-time and hand them food through the gates. You were always comparing your food with your mates. I was in the jam section – I never made it to the cheese on toast section.

But my most embarrassing moment at school was going to the baths.

Like a lot of kids, I didn't have a cozzie – (swimming costume) and so I used to have to go in the baths with no cozzie on.

We used to finish morning school at noon and we had to walk 500 yards out of the school gate to get to the centre where they served the food.

We used to run out of that gate like Olympic athletes.

If Linford Christie had been in our class, we certainly would have given him a run for his money.

We seemed to have the mistaken idea that if you got there early you got more food, but it wasn't the case. The queue was massive and there was no way you could bunk in or save a place for your mates.

Scouse, Spam, and Sago. I actually liked school dinners, but not the puddings – they were horrible. I never remember Scouse being as thick as we had it at school – how they could even get the ladle in the pot, I'll never know.

And those sausages, you could have used them in a fight they were like deadly weapons.

But even though they were crunchy I really enjoyed them.

We used to watch the dinner ladies like hawks when they were cutting up cakes or the pies to make sure the lad in front of you didn't get more than his fair share.

I used to love those big steak and kidney pies in steel trays that they used to cut into squares. They had a thick crust and gravy.

You used to be dead lucky when you got the last bit in the tray and they used to scrape off all the bits that had stuck to the sides and put them on your plate. We used to have Spam about three times a week with red-hot gravy.

My biggest dislikes and I believed everyone reading this book will say the same – tapioca.

We called it frogspawn. And that was closely followed by sago. It didn't even taste as good as wallpaper paste.

There was always a big splodge of jam in the middle – it looked like a mass of blood.

I hated butterbeans too . . . they tasted like sawdust.

The cheese pie – well, I could go on, that tasted horrible and was a funny shade of red.

But the roasties were brilliant. They did great roasties at my school. I only wish the jackets had been as good.

Other than that the only veggies I can recall were peas.

We thought broccoli was a place in Spain.

All the dinner ladies had red rosy faces. They wore hats and they always looked very clean.

I often think about the blancmange. They didn't look like the ones you had in comics. In comics they stood proud and looked back at you. School blancmange in real life always crumbled and collapsed and slopped all over the place.

The really strong memory of school food was the smell – no matter what the food was it ALWAYS seemed to smell of Scouse.

It's funny now but we never seemed to get fish.

We never had roast beef either. The salads were terrible, too. I think they used all the stuff they didn't put in the cheese pie . . .

SCOFF AND SWEETS

There was hardly ever butter in our house, always marge.

But when we did have butter it was never just called 'butter'. It was always best butter.

The day would start with breakfast and that was always Kellogg's or Puffed Wheat.

And the boxes they came in always seemed gigantic.

Your mam would empty them out into the bowl and no matter how much she poured out there was always a huge pile left.

When you had finished with the box you could use the paper inside to wrap up your dinner for school or you could use it to trace with.

The business about competition between shops is nothing new. They talk about price wars between supermarkets now. But it was just as strong when we were kids.

My mam used to send me to the corner of Atwell Street, which was about half a mile away to get the fish and chips, and the reason was they did 'specials'.

You could get one of their specials – which could be fish, chips and peas – for sixpence.

Your mam would know which chippies had special offers on which you always had two all to the best even if it was miles away.

Once you had finished the fish and chips, there were little crispy bits at the bottom.

They had a special name for them because you could get a bag full for about a penny. But I can't remember what we called them.

You used to be able to get lovely pink, penny spearmint bars too.

If you sucked them and then pulled them out of your mouth they would stretch about eight feet in front of your face before they broke off.

I used to love porridge on a cold morning. My Granny

THE EARLY YEARS...

The Family:
About 1953. Dot, Joan,
Billy, Stephen, Eilleen

Not forgotten:
Only picture I ever saw of my Dad –
and only a few memories

Happiness:
Camping in
North Wales
with one of my
pals, in 1959

July, 1958.

WILLIAM GEORGE BUTLER entered the School in
September 1953. He has recently been sitting
for the General Certificate of Education
Examination (Ordinary Level) in English Language,
French, Mathematics and Physics. He has also
studied History, Latin and Chemistry.

He has shown average ability and industry. His
behaviour has been satisfactory but he needs to
exert himself more. He is reliable in character
and I can recommend him.

He has played in our Third Football XI and taken
part in Cross Country Running.

K. Croft

Headmaster.

Just for the record:
One of my old school
reports from Liverpool
Collegiate, 1958

Dancing Feet:
On stage at Hollyoak with
Mersey Beats' Billy Kinsley
in the background, 1964

A face for radio:
Only existing photo of the Tuxedos at the Cavern
in the 60s and my face is blocked out! TYPICAL

Caught in the act: Never could pick shirts. At Radio Merseyside, 1976

OH BOY!: With Buddy Holly's manager Norman Petty also in 1976

Moptops:
Given the brush off with cleaners at the Port of Liverpool building in 1980

Bow-brunnell:
My neck attached by a Bat! At the Huyton Suite for a Country Music night surrounded by some fans, 1976

POSER: Why did Wally put super-glue in my pocket?

Great hair: A failed Steptoe audition

T-shirt shame ~~ut the hair: day at Radio in 1979

A race picture:
My 'Everton have won' face!
Publicity shot 1982

Enough to turn you to drink:
Billy's beer price protest. VAT and Tax battle in 1976

Post show pint:
the good old brown
mixed, publicity shot
from 1988

Potty about radio:
Will it fit under the [
I was granted
Merseysider of the
Month in April, 1985

Love the turn ups:
Pilot of the airwaves at
Radio Merseyside . . .
again, 1988

used to make the porridge and if we were lucky enough to have a tin of syrup we would have it in the porridge and it was wonderful.

And when my mam wasn't looking I used to put syrup on my Kellogs, but the trouble was you only got one spoonful because the syrup would make them all stick together in one lump.

I still love Christmas pudding today as much as I did when I was a kid.

But the thrill was gone because there is no money in it now. I don't think people put money in it anymore?

It used to amaze me that your Mam could always make sure everyone got some money.

It always baffled me how she knew where the money was so she could make sure we all got some.

She used to get at me, too.

When I was always looking at the pictures on the front of the biscuits. Do you remember them?

They had illustrations of children skipping or on a swing and my Mam would say: "Are you going to eat those biscuits? Or just read them?"

The things we used to put on butties would astound people today:

Conny onny butties . . .

Sugar butties

But my favourite was the HP Sauce buttie.

Looking back there were some strange things on food bottles and packets then. Camp Coffee bottles had a picture of an English officer and a slave on the front.

HP Sauce bottles had the Houses of Parliament on.

But the strangest of all was Quaker Puffed Wheat.

On top of that packet it said 'Shot from guns' and to this day I don't know why I used to have a picture of this huge cannon with all this puffed out wheat coming out of it.

But Sunday dinner was the big thing. Everybody had it at one o'clock.

The street would be deserted because everybody had his or her dinner at the same time.

Everything seemed so cheap then, to buy that is.

There were stacks of things you could buy at the shop for a penny then:

ABC chewing gum

Sambo (never PC) chewy

They wouldn't allow it these days and besides it made your tongue and teeth go black.

Bobby which was really sweet . . . dolly mixtures, gob stoppers . . . the list goes on.

FRIENDS... AND FOES

Mates are the people you always say you'll never lose touch with but, most of the time, you do.

Yet you actually talk about them most of your adult life.

I'd love to see some of my old mates and talk to them about childhood memories.

Those who can answer you back – apart from your mum and dad. Real mates are those you have before you hit 15.

The mates you used to call in to see after you had had your dinner.

My nickname was bunner because Billy Butler is BB – the same initials as Bugs Bunny.

The one I felt sorry for in our gang – which consisted of me, Albert Myers and Bobby Thomas – his nickname was Judas.

It couldn't have been much fun to be called Judas when you are a kid.

The reason he was given that name was when one of us broke a window playing footy he told on us.

Snitched . . .

Mates had real gangs then like a cowboy posse.

We all had an agreement that if anyone was ever in

trouble there'd be a gang scream or a gang yell. A certain sound – no matter where you were . . . your mates would have to come.

But they never did, I was always the unlucky one.

We once bunked into the Royal picture house, which had a high cash till you could crawl under.

Albert did – and then I did and then I heard someone shouting: "Where are you going . . . where are you going?"

I sat petrified in that aisle until the end of the picture for about two and half hours.

On the way out Albert and Bobby were both standing with the manager and when I came out they said: "That's him . . ."

I never spoke to them for days.

They snitched.

But you forgot things like that when you were mates.

There were always regular fights to see who was 'cock of our gang' and it was usually me.

Every now and then, Albert Myers would beat me but we could both beat Bobby.

Once Bobby came up to me and said: "I want to fight yer, because I think I can beat yer NOW."

Then he ran towards me with his arm twirling like a windmill and he ran right at me and I just hit him in the stomach.

That was typical of gangs always up to something. Always caught doing things.

Albert Myers and me were caught after setting fire to some woman's bin when the bins were set into the wall.

His mam then said I couldn't play with him because I was a bad influence.

And there I was left standing in the street with no place to go.

Albert and I had this mate called Kevin Howard.

He had a great set of Dinky motors and we'd go to his house to see them.

He had about 20 cars, but by the time we left he had about five left.

Yeah and all five would have a tyre missing . . .

NEW YEAR'S EVE

People really knew how to welcome in the New Year.

New Year's Eve was a much bigger event on the social calendar – a night when communities joined together in mass celebration.

Parties seemed to be going on in every other house and once the New Year had been let in, the streets came alive as revellers danced and sang into the wee small hours.

As children it was the ideal opportunity to stay up late and join in the fun with the grown ups.

I remember we always went out into the street and waited for the Ogden Tobacco Company's big clock to chime.

That's what saddens me about New Year these days – everyone seems to celebrate indoors.

Years ago it was always outside in the street.

You were outside your house and your neighbours were outside theirs and then you joined together and danced in a big ring.

I didn't mind the thought of a new year coming, but what I hated was the stroke of 12, because everyone tried to kiss you.

It was all the neighbours you didn't know and aunties and uncles.

I didn't like anyone kissing me.

When you were actually outside you always headed for the nearest lamppost so you could be under the light.

I always remember people being nice to people they hated.

They were all benevolent to people they couldn't stand

and the next day things went back to normal.

You'd go inside and there'd be loads of wooden crates of ale stacked on top of each other.

I couldn't understand all these people drinking this stuff. I took a sip once and it was horrible.

Don't times change?

But my grandad could knock it back. I loved the tale about how he went abroad and when he came back he had to pay duty on his breath.

I used to hate being sent to bed only an hour into New Year because I used to always get told by my mates that after a few ales everyone would get really generous and say: "Here you are son, here's some money for the New Year."

But when I could stay up, some of my uncles would get a shilling out and say: "Guess heads or tails correctly and you can have it."

And they'd add: "Have a silver shilling."

But you couldn't have anything else – there were no copper shillings."

New Year's Day was no big deal in itself.

There were no resolutions made or anything.

You just saw it as a day when there would be a good footy match.

Everton always seemed to have a big match, normally against Man United.

New Year's Eve was the big day.

From the moment you got up, you would be as good as gold so your mam would let you stay up late.

The singing would start early because you've got to remember the pubs shut at 10pm.

And there'd always be someone on your front door step singing their heads off at 11pm because they had had too much ale in the pub and they were killing time for midnight.

I used to sing My Happiness but only if they shut the

kitchen door and I could sing it from the bottom of the lobby.

Then, when I'd finished, the door would open and everyone would clap.

Once my aunties and uncles asked me to put a show on for them. I said 'OK'.

I went through to the back kitchen to get ready.

I'd seen Al Jolson at the pictures doing Sonny Boy, so I blacked up using gravy browning. I got it all over my shirt, but it was worth it because I got half a crown off my Uncle Paddy.

I got in trouble though. The next morning, because I went to bed with it on, it was all on my pillow.

The only time I can remember letting the New Year in was, if I am not mistaken, the year when Man City knocked out Liverpool in the FA Cup.

Grandad, a big RED blamed me for his team getting beat because it was me who let the New Year in.

And I still want to know dear reader, is there . . . is there anyone who knows the second verse of Auld Lang Syne?

I don't . . .

HEROES

My first football heroes were Lanky Hutton, Bernard Briggs Nick Smith and Arnold Tabbs in the Rover, Adventure and Wizard comics.

Bernard Briggs went a whole season without letting a goal in. Lanky Hutton won the league and the cup and saved more penalties than any other goalie in comics, and Nick Smith was the only footballer who had one leg shorter than the other and still captained England.

I don't think there was the same thrill when I got to idolise real football heroes.

Reading the local and national papers was never as

exciting as reading the Rover, Adventure or the Hotspur.

But another of my heroes was Flash Gordon. I believe he is very old now and people call him Gordon.

I wanted to be a spaceman when I grew up and there's still a chance of that. We would go to the Saturday matinees to watch Flash go into space and visit strange planets.

That was what we played on the streets. I used to paint lightning on my vest in black lead. I'd wet the pencil so it would go blue and draw a streak down it. Then I'd paint a stripe down my footie kecks and that was my Flash Gordon outfit.

Back on earth football produced many heroes. Liverpool had a centre-half called Dick White who scored more own goals than any player in living memory – and he had a chin that made Jimmy Hill's look flat. The players then didn't even have glamorous names.

Today you've got Arteta, Torres, Pienaar – Dick White and Fred Morris didn't have the same ring to them.

There weren't football magazines galore in which you could build up heroes. They were only in the Saturday and Sunday papers with pictures of football in.

The first sporting hero I can remember influencing me was Dennis Compton, because he made me buy Brylcream. He used to advertise it I think.

Then there was another fellow whose name I can't remember who advertised Trugel – which didn't leave greasy stains on the back of the chair.

CHILDHOOD

Our Gang – (me, Albert and Bobby) had an agreement that if we were caught doing anything wrong by the authority, when asked, we would give the wrong names in.

It so happened that a policeman caught us stealing

turnips (only the big stuff for us) from a farmer's field in Cantril farm.

As arranged when the policeman took out his notebook he asked for Bobby's name, Bobby said: "Norman Brown, 32 Severs Street, Liverpool 6."

When he asked me I said: "Dave Bently, 8 Compton Street, Liverpool 6."

Then he asked Albert and Albert replied: "Billy Butler, 52 Grey Rock Street, Liverpool 6."

You should have seen my face.

He gave MY name and address.

My face was a picture! the policeman said he would be be calling to see our parents and told us to go home.

I said to Albert: "You gave him my name and address?"

Albert replied "Well, you said give him the wrong name and address and that's NOT mine!"

WINTERS

The amazing thing is that children who are under 10 now don't know what winter really is.

How many of today's kids have had the wonderful experience of building a snowman or even having snow one day and it still being there the next?

When I was a kid we used to pray for snow.

I recall kneeling for my prayers at night and saying God Bless my mama and dad and then saying, "Please let it snow . . ."

You'd be at school and you'd look out of the window and see it had started to snow and you'd be saying to yourself "Please let it stick, please let it stick."

But you would also have this fear that if you looked out of the window again it would have stopped.

The snow even stuck to the cracks in the walls where the cement was.

Snowing would also mean extra money.

There were the snow shifters who had real spades, then there were people like me and me mates who had to use their mam's coal shovels.

The trouble was that when you used the shovel to try and cut through the ice the edge would bend up and you'd be in lumber because your mam wouldn't be able to get it under the slack in the coal place.

After a few winters, you knew the best houses to go for snow shifting, but there was always the problem of knowing if you should just do the step, or the step and the path, or the garden or even the pavement.

There was also the terrible time when you'd do the entire shifting and then knock on the door and say: "Hey mister, I've cleared the snow," and they'd just say. "Thanks."

And shut the door. That happened to me once and we went back that night and . . . put the snow back.

Another thing the kids of today haven't experienced, because we rarely get that level of snow anymore – and even if we did there would be too many cars to do it – is making slides.

Those amazing slides you would make and they'd be right in the middle of the road.

You would take this huge run up to the start of the slide before you hit it.

If there had been an interest in ski-ing then, some of the kids in our street would have won gold medals.

But I always fell over and I would end up going home with a massive lump on my head.

Winters will always remind me of snowball fights – they were wonderful.

I was hopeless, but Kevin Caphrey was in our gang and he could hit you at 45 yards.

Your mam would always make you put your gloves on if you were going out in the snow.

But you couldn't throw snowballs properly with gloves on, so you would have to take them off and use your bare hands and they would get freezing. We would make giant snowballs starting with a little one at the top of the street or in Newsham Park.

You'd end up with a massive ball in the end and you would just leave it there. Some of them would take two or three people to push and they would end up in the middle of the road and cars had to drive around them.

I used to love getting up first thing in the morning when we had snow and looking back at my footprints across the yard.

I loved twanging the washing line because it would always have a thin layer of snow on it and you'd twang it and it would go right up in the air.

That time of year always makes me think of winter warmers.

There were tins of which you would knock holes in with a nail, put a page of a newspaper at the bottom, fill it with wood, set fire to the paper then swing it round my head.

They must have been one of my early introductions to DIY disasters.

I made my own winter warmer but made the fatal mistake of using string instead of wire to swing it around.

I was twirling it round and it came off and went right through Number 11's window and I nearly set the front parlour on fire.

When it was really cold and some kid came up behind me and flicked my ear. Oooh . . . the pain was terrible and it would seem to last all day.

If you had a balaclava on it would protect your ears as well as keep you warm.

In school we would be sitting there with coats on, balaclavas and gloves.

And then they'd give you frozen milk and you'd try and get to the great big central heating pipes to sit on them to get warm and wait for your frozen milk to melt.

BUSES & TRAINS

Getting around where you lived when you were kids was always a fun adventure.

The buses I used to get when I was young were the 75 to my Aunty Dorothy's in Huyton, otherwise known as Dovecot, and the 19a to Goodison Park, and I think it was the 11 to Cantril Farm to look for conkers.

You could always get return fares of course and it would be horrible if you lost the ticket.

The number of times me and my mates would be looking in the gutters picking up tickets and examining them just in case it was a return you could use to get home.

There were loads of inspectors then.

And they always seemed to get on YOUR bus. They were ogres. Those two words "TICKETS PLEASE" were terrifying to us when they rang out on the top deck and you didn't have one.

Then there was the adult ticket and one they used to call a scholar.

The scholar was obviously cheaper. I think I got a scholar ticket until I was 27.

I left the Collegiate when I was 15 and kept my school hat to wear on the buses.

Up until I was 17 I was going into town wearing my Collegiate hat and was asking for a half-fare.

In those days bus conductors were real characters.

Some of them would walk up and down singing or cracking jokes.

They would know all the passengers by name.

And some of the passengers were characters were too.

I had to get buses because I have no sense of direction then, as now.

So whenever I got on a bus I would have to ask the conductor to tell me where my stop was.

I used to hate travelling on buses simply because I couldn't relax for a minute.

I couldn't read or anything, in case I missed him shouting my stop.

There was one art form called skipping off. Some fellers could skip off and run backwards and still carry on a conversation with someone on the platform.

Then there were other people who were terrible at skipping off, they would skip off and go hurtling into the front of a shop or into a queue.

The most embarrassing thing was running for a bus and then not getting it.

You'd be running along with your arms outstretched ready to grab the pole and it would gradually pull away from you.

I used to keep running and pretend I wasn't going for a bus at all, that I was just out for a run.

Eventually getting on . . . going upstairs on a bus used to be like going into World War II smog. The smoke was that dense.

Another transport we used was the Overhead Railway. Wally loved that because he helped to build it . . .

The ferries were great too. I used to love it when we'd race down the tunnel towards the floating terminal.

Your legs were a blur.

I always felt that you wouldn't stop before you ran into the Mersey.

And it always seemed so enormously crowded. There was always a big queue pushing you onto the boat.

I used to marvel at the way the man in the ferry could always drop the gangway right on the steel line.

If you stood one inch behind the line he'd still get it straight on the mark and not hit anyone.

Looking back we always used to go to Moreton. The ferry to Birkenhead and then the bus to Moreton.

Moreton wasn't that many miles away. Yet I knew people

who went on holiday there.

From Liverpool.

They took tents and stayed there for a week and sent postcards home. It's funny how things change.

When I was a kid my ambition was to ride in the sidecar of a motorbike.

You wouldn't be seen dead in one nowadays.

Motorbikes fascinated me. The ones around when we were kids were massive things covered in chrome.

When they had a sidecar on it gave them a romantic image to me.

Years ago fellers brought their girls home in the side-car of a motorbike.

CHRISTMAS

We didn't have a Christmas tree in our house but it was always a happy and exciting time of the year.

It's easy for kids today to make their present lists out for Father Christmas because there are endless adverts on the telly.

So they just tend to say, "I want that or that. AND that."

Our lists were made up of things we had seen in toy shop windows or in our mam's Littlewoods or Grattan catalogues.

Our 'home grotto' when we were kids was the catalogue.

Unlike Wally Scott, I went straight to the toy section and he went to the women's underwear.

We would go round the toyshops and press our noses against the window. You see a toy and say to your mate: "I claim that one and he'd say: "You're too late, I've already claimed that one."

I can still picture my Uncle Paddy or Aunty Ruth saying, once it got into December, "Now what do you want Father Christmas to bring you?"

And you'd end up talking for about five minutes telling them all the things you would like.

It was easy then, when Christmas was coming, to get us kids to be good. If we were naughty Mam would say, "Father Christmas is listening" and you'd stop.

But if things got really bad she'd stick her head up the chimney and yell: "Father Christmas, do you know what these two are doing down here?" and we'd say: "Don't tell him mam, please don't tell him."

Around October, I remember I would join a sweet club and put two pence or three pence a week in until Christmas. In the end I'd get a tin of Sharp's toffees.

Just after I'd lost my mam, I actually found an old sweet club card of mine and the tin of sweets was 2s and 6d and I had put my final 2d down on December 22 after saving up since October.

It brought a tear to my eye and I've kept the card just to show the days when money really was a struggle and it took a long time to get as little as 2s 6d.

One way we did make money was by going carol singing and we'd start about December the first. There used to be areas where you would be going on other gangs' territories.

It wasn't like today when kids knock on your door and ask if you'd like them to sing a carol.

We'd sing two or three, then we'd knock on the door and then you'd start to panic because you'd sung three or four carols for nothing and they hadn't answered the door.

So you'd open the letter box and shout through "Happy Christmas, Missus!"

Once I even took a wind up gramophone and some 78 Christmas records and I thought I was going to make a fortune but it didn't work out.

Some of the grottos that the stores in town had in those days were great.

Blackler's was fantastic with the most magnificent giant Father Christmas and Lewis's had a wonderful grotto. I can still picture the dancing waters in TJ Hughes.

The grottos were magic places then, you'd be in them for a good five or six minutes just looking around.

We even had grotto days at school – days when you were let off just to go to the grotto and there were always massive queues when you arrived at the shop.

When it came to decorating the house I used to try and get out of it because we had to make our own decorations, paper chains and things.

The only thing that had been bought were those round Christmas paper bells, which would open out, and they'd last for years and years.

On Christmas Day there was only a fraction of the money available for parents to spend on pressies but there was plenty of festive fun.

Christmas Day would really start when it was dead dark.

You'd wake up at the bottom of the bed with your foot to see if that empty pillowslip had now got lumpy bits in it.

There would be a Christmas stocking as well because that was what Father Christmas would put your nuts and sweets and fruit in. Between 5am and 7am on Christmas morning all over the country you would be able to hear the same two words.

"He's been."

I recall how we used to break the nuts. It was on the back kitchen floor. We didn't have any carpet or anything like that, just tiles – black and red tiles.

All over Christmas the back kitchen floor would be littered with bits of nuts after we'd used the old iron on the nut. The iron would render the nut completely useless really and you would just have to scrape up what bits you had left.

These days everyone has nutcrackers.

I think they should supply you with dynamite for the almonds because there's no nutcracker ever made that can crack an almond.

The best present I remember receiving when I was a kid was a double barrel pop gun.

It had two corks which doubled the firepower and you could fire them one at a time.

The problem with pop guns tended to be that, after just a day, one of your springs snapped, or you had lost your cork.

I think the cat hated the pop gun most. I am sorry to say this, but the cat was the first thing you shot with your pop gun.

In fact anything that fired missiles was aimed at the cat.

Cats everywhere please forgive me.

It even didn't matter if the cat hid under the sideboard, you'd still be able to aim it.

There were also toys that fired matchsticks. The thing I could never understand about those matchstick guns was why it was so hard to pull back the little wire to make it fire. You needed the strength of about ten men to do it.

Everyone must have got a compendium of games.

It seemed to work out that the more games you had in the box, the cheaper it seemed to be.

All the toys were 'wind up' then and after about a week you would have over-wound them and bust the springs or you would have lost the keys.

There was nothing worse than walking around with a toy that didn't have a key.

One of my favourite toys was the conductor's set you used to get. They were brilliant.

I'd make my mam, aunts and uncles sit in a line on the couch and I'd walk along saying: "FARES PLEASE. Going to town?"

"Right, that's two pence."

And the outfit came with a ticket machine and a hat and badge. It was great.

I remember seeing the illuminated much-loved tram that toured the Liverpool streets over the festive season.

Back home, my mam used to be really good at hiding the presents. I don't ever recall being able to find them.

I'd search the house from top to bottom but never find them.

I hated getting anything as a present that I had to build, because I just couldn't do it.

It must have been a pointer to my future life.

Every year you used to get a selection box – Santa's bumper selection box, all full of different sweets.

And dominoes every year. I always seemed to get them.

And green soldiers . . . thousands of these great soldiers.

We were daft as kids if you got footy boots for Christmas, you would actually go out in them . . .

And your shorts.

They had cork studs and big steel toe-caps, but you'd go out in them and call for your mates.

My mates always seemed to get a black board and chalks or dolls.

I can trace the way dolls improved each year from the ones that just said, 'Mammy' when you held them upside down to the ones that walked along with you when you held their hand.

One thing I hated about Christmas was mistletoe. I stayed well away from that stuff.

I'd hop it if my aunties came around or the little girl from down the road came in.

The problem was, my aunties used to carry some round with them and they'd always end up catching you.

Christmas Day itself seemed to last forever.

We didn't have a telly then – so you played all day.

If you'd been given a game you played them all day with your parents and brothers and sisters.

Today it is so different. Plasma screens, even tellys on mobile phones, computers, I-pods, I-pads. The kids seem to spend all of their time in front of a screen because you need a telly or computer to play most of their games.

We had blow football and snakes and ladders and we'd go mad if we went down the ladder.

Oh, and Christmas dinner was a big part of the day.

We'd been living with my mam and grandad so there would be eight of us sat down. I think we had chicken rather than turkey. But chicken then was a big luxury not an everyday food like today.

They were real Holly days . . . last year I walked half a mile to get some batteries about 10am on Christmas Day.

Didn't see any kid playing out with presents. How sad.

COMICS

Comics – just not stand ups but the paper kind. I loved them and still do.

I used to go to Rayners on West Derby Road and they used to have all the new comics in layers with just their titles showing.

The one I remember the most was called Chips and it had two tramps Wearie Willie and Tired Tim.

The comics I got back then were the Rover, the Wizard the Adventure and the Hotspur.

The Beano and The Dandy were like the picture comics but the Rover and the Wizard were all stories.

There were characters called Andrew Glenn and Black Bob. He was in the Dandy and drawn by Dudley D Watkins – it was also in the Sunday Post.

Watkins was famous because he also did the William Books and 'Oor Wullie'

Andrew Glenn looked like president Abraham Lincoln.

To me Black Bob used to make Skippy the kangaroo seem dyslexic. He was always finding lambs lost in the snow. He was one of them dogs that could do anything, but

I bet he couldn't beg. There were some super characters in Hotspur and The Adventure.

Morgyn the Mighty was one – that comic's strong man.

He was an enormously powerful man – he made Hercules seem like a wimp.

They also had boxing stories as well and I learnt a lot about boxers from that comic.

In fact, I got most of my knowledge about the Second World War because I read a series called 'I Flew with Braddock' – his co-pilot George Bourne told his story.

There were always great stories about monsters in the Wizard and the Hotspur.

You had to use your imagination.

The one I remember most was this massive mountain somewhere in England and you realised it wasn't a mountain – it was this dinosaur that had been asleep for millions of years.

And it suddenly woke up.

There was also one about the giant cactus in Hyde Park.

And they had to send jets and rockets against it because it was firing off these massive quills against all kinds of cities and countries and everything.

And you lived it.

I lived in fear of cactuses and I was scared to climb up any mountains just in case it turned into a dinosaur.

In Film Fun whenever anyone fainted they would faint about eight foot off the ground.

Film Fun would usually have Laurel and Hardy on the front cover and they would always be down and out on their luck.

By the end they'd always end up eating with someone who'd have a huge tie and gold tie pin.

The hotel was always the Hotel De Swank or Hotel De Posh and the meal was a very, very, very big plate of mashed potato with sausages sticking out of the end.

That was always the slap up meal.

All the crooks had bags with swag written on the side, a mask and a red and white striped jumper.

Comics always had brilliant drawings of treasure.

The pirate stories with the treasure chest. It was always over-flowing with money, jewels and goblets.

I always used to dream of finding some of that treasure.

FUN AND GAMES

Kids can't play games in the street like we did any more because of the traffic.

It just couldn't be done today.

Football was the big thing and we used to play across the street and use the gardens as goals. But you had to try and pick a garden with trees because then you wouldn't break the windows if you hammered the ball in.

Many's the time I went home with bad knees after diving full length to tip the ball round the post – the end of the garden wall.

The people who always spoilt street games were the cheats, there was always one in every gang, always the fellers who, when they were counting up to 100 in hide and seek, would always look out of the side of their arm to see where you were running.

Or they would count it in tens instead of ones.

There were always those neighbours who would tell you to "go and play at your own end."

They did this especially if you were playing hop scotch and you had to chalk squares, one to nine, on the pavements, because you would always chalk it outside someone else's house NEVER your own.

Everything you needed for games then were all around you.

For hopscotch, all you needed was a bit of old plaster for the chalk and a bit of slate and you had a game going.

At night the only place you could play in the street was by the lamp-post. And what did every lamp-post have around it?

An old bicycle tyre.

The game where I got the most injuries was skipping.

You could tie one end of the rope to the garden fence and someone would stand by the gutter turning it. But it was the jumping in bit I could never get.

You would have to run in while it was turning. The rope was supposed to go under your feet, but with me it was always on the nose – it always hit me right on my hooter.

You could play loads of games with a rope. It was a lasso.

And you used it for that other game, higher and higher, where you stretched the rope and had to jump over.

You would end up taking your run-up from half way down the street to try and get over it.

The girls were really great at skipping. They could do it crossing their arms as they were going.

Chalk was essential – you could play loads of games just with a piece of chalk.

You just couldn't have had a game of cricket without chalk.

You used it to draw the crease and draw the wickets on the wall.

It was the only way you could be sure if someone was out because you could look at the ball to see if there was a white mark on where it had hit the wicket.

There were special rules for street cricket – you could catch it with one hand off a wall and six was over the garden wall.

Once I scored 135 not out. I went in and told my mam. I was made up – 135 not out.

There were special ways of picking sides. You would put your left foot in a circle and all your mates would, too.

And you would count round the feet, saying: "Your shoes are dirty, please change your feet."

The one it stopped at would have to put his other foot in and out, if the other foot got done, you were out.

TRADERS

These characters seemed to be everywhere – and yet now they just don't exist at that level anymore – they were probably what we'd now call the 'black economy'.

They just disappeared.

Local stars such as the rag and bone man, laden with a bag full of dubious 'prizes'.

There were bookies runners who secretly took bets.

There were people who sang for a few coppers then the others who would have quite a few coppers chasing them.

I remember there'd be a knock on the door: "Hello, Mrs B, do you want your scissors sharpening?"

There would be this little man with a wheel. I used to love to watch all the sparks that would belt out as he sharpened the knives.

I was made up when he came to the door – we'd have these dead sharp knives and I could cut up the orange boxes and make them into swords.

There was another feller called the Salt Man.

He would stand in the street and shout 'SALT' dead loud.

There'd be people, walking up and own the entry singing – not in the street – but in the entry and ma would say to me: "Ere go and give that feller a penny, son."

I'd go back and give him a penny.

Yer mams never had much money but they always find time to give those fellers a few spare coppers.

Then we had the bookies runner.

There would be two blokes who would stand at either end of the entry and keep a look out for police because it was illegal then. If the police had a runner your house was always open to them.

One bloke running through our house said to me mam: "Sorry about this Gladys," and I'd be sitting there thinking "Who the hell was that?"

My grandad would give me the money and on this piece of paper was the name 'George Glasses.' A lot of grandparents would send you to the man on the corner and I'd believe it would be for the weekend's meat. I always thought that the bookie was a butcher.

The best street traders of the lot were the rag and bone men. Most parents and grandparents probably hated them.

It was the only way some kids could get any toys.

I'd ask: "Any rags, mam?"

She'd say "No". Then I'd go upstairs and pull a few things out and say: "What about these?"

And she'd look at me and say: "They are NOT rags."

Fair game for the rag and bone man were blankets on the bed.

He would have this big bag of toys but they didn't seem to be worth anything.

He must have made a fortune because he offered us a load of rubbish.

The worst was a tin frog.

A clocking tin frog made of cheap tin – it had a steel extension and when you pressed it the thing clicked.

And there was a skewy type thing with a pair of wings.

Yet, to us, the rag and bone man was like Father Christmas.

You could get aircraft goggles and pretend to be a pilot but the plastic would cut into your nose.

We never knew what the rag man was shouting . . . it must have been something with rags in it.

There were also the blokes who turned up with a pair of

shears and they'd say to me mam: "Can I cut your trees, missus?"

They would never clean up after them.

I used to love cleaning up all those leaves.

I'd love it – strange – but you'd help anyone in those days . . . as long as it wasn't your mam and dad.

You weren't allowed to do anything on Sundays.

You couldn't play football, in the end you usually had to find a schoolyard and climb over the gate and play there.

But so much for being 'quiet'.

How was that possible? I don't know how because there would be a Boys Brigade band marching up the street.

Sometimes you'd hear the strains of them, five streets away, and you'd be trying to guess where they were and in which direction they were going.

And then you would be out following the band and you'd get lost.

The number of times I got lost on a Sunday morning is legendary.

Another thing about Sundays was you had to wear your Sunday Best. I had to wear a tie and my short pants and I've got terrible legs.

Your socks had to be pulled up as well. You'd keep them up with elastic.

And there were always set times on a Sunday.

If ever you wanted something sweet like a lolly-ice you had to get it before twelve.

Shops were always shut in the afternoons.

Dinner was always at one o'clock.

You had to wait for your dad or, in my case, my grandad, to come back from the pub.

He'd bring a bottle of brown home and still manage to get five shandies out of it for the kids.

And your tea was always at five o'clock.

But the worst thing was that we had to go to Sunday school.

My first real introduction was reading out of the Bible about blind Bartimeus.

Sitting on the highway begging.

What religion you were didn't enter into it.

But it did have its good points because you could always have a laugh at the way teachers sang.

When you are a kid, grown-ups sing in very funny voices.

There were also days out for treats.

SUNDAYS

They took us to Helsby once a year on a coach.

I love my relatives and Aunts and Uncles used to come around on a Sunday.

The only annoying thing was that if they came when you were at Sunday School you'd miss out on sixpence or a shilling as a gift.

On Sundays there'd always be the 'pitch and toss' fellas outside the pub.

I used to wonder what game they were playing.

They'd give you a few pennies to keep look out because gambling was illegal.

I loved radio on a Sunday

I liked Life with the Nylons, Tony Hancock and Max Bygraves who were both in Educating Archie . . . so was Julie Andrews. Then there was Down Your Way and In Town Tonight.

The Billy Cotton Band Show always started with Wakey Wakey. Billy Cotton's Piece De Resistance was The Dambusters march.

He used to play it every week.

I knew every note of it.

But Sundays meant you had to have a bath. I never understood the logic of having a bath on a Sunday because you'd be in your clean clothes all day.

In our case it was a tin bath in front of the fire.

The dread used to be when there was a knock and your mam would go to the door and you'd hear someone coming up the hall and you would desperately be looking for a flannel to cover yourself up.

DREADING THINGS

My mam would say if you don't wash your face and if you don't do it properly I'LL do it.

Not once did you escape from your mam's clutches.

I'm sure that's why I've got a bald patch now – my mam rubbed my hair off.

And there were yer mam's repairs.

You had to stand in front of her while she sewed a button on your fly and you still had your trousers on.

You were scared to move in case she got you with this huge darning needle.

It was a lethal weapon.

That same terror was there when she sewed a button on your shirt collar – you were scared she would lance your Adam's Apple.

My mam would put her head round the barber's door on Saturday mornings when the adults were in and she'd say: "D'yer do kids today?"

And he'd say: "Oh, bring him in."

All you could remember was masses of hair falling off your shoulders – no technique just those huge shears.

Your fear was tempered, though, because the barber had comics to read.

Then there was the chance to watch the barber burn the bloke's hair off at the back of his head.

He'd set light to a taper and burn off their hair.

There was the CLINIC – that word struck fear into us kids and as you were going in you always saw those kids coming out with purple over their faces.

I still dread the very word 'Clinic'. You'd come out with a note for your mam.

You knew you had something but you didn't know what. Usually it was nits.

More dread came at the swimming baths.

If you forgot your cozzie you had to go in yer skins – nothing on.

I hated that, especially afterwards and the showers.

Dancing – now that was another dread.

You'd sit in a circle and girls would have to pick someone. You would look away . . . feign infections, look ugly – anything.

At home, I hated going down to the cellar for coal just as much.

There was no lighting so I would go down there with a candle convinced it was full of cockroaches. Giant Spiders scared the life out of me.

And when the coalman hadn't been, mam would ask me to go and shovel under the cellar stairs.

Getting ill or breaking something was a dread. You would end up with plaster around your arm and leg – four tonnes of it set by Wimpy.

What about going for the messages . . . to the shops without a note. I'd start off with it all in my head.

A quarter of billed ham, a bottle of milk. I'd be saying it all the way to the shops. Then, when I got home, I'd end up saying: "Mam, what was it you wanted?"

Me mam once sent me out for a packet of ciggies and I couldn't remember the brand she liked. I asked: "What happens if they haven't got them?"

She said: "Get me anything."

They didn't have them so I got a meat pie.

RADIO DAYS

It was called the wireless – never the radio. There was no telly so you had to use your imagination.

There were programmes you would just not listen to.

There was Music While You Work and as soon as the music came on you'd find somewhere else to be.

Or, when Mrs Dale's diary came on and you never heard us listening to the Archers.

On Saturday mornings we would listen to children's requests – I first heard the Burl Ives and his song There Was an Old Lady. Who can forget Nellie The Elephant – such classics.

But I never heard a request from the north. As Wally pointed out they were for the south and I think that's because nobody sent them in thinking they would get skitted for writing in.

The reception in our house wasn't too good so I'd go up to Mrs Hatch's to hear children's hour.

When I was 11 and growing up there was one great one for us kids called Johnny Into Space.

It was like Star Trek has now become for the television age.

That's what was great about the wireless – imagination.

I loved Dick Barton Special Agent. That theme music called The Devil's Gallop and those endings, such as, will Jock escape? and will Snowy be there in time?

Most of the great radio shows came on at 7pm but I'd have to be in bed by then.

So I'd go upstairs and be good.

I'd sing my youngest brother and sister to sleep and then be able to go downstairs and listen to Over The Garden Wall, Take it From Here and Have a Go with Wilfred Pickles.

I also loved Educating Archie – it never occurred to us that it was a ventriloquist on the wireless.

He used to have new tutors all the time – such as Tony Hancock and Julie Andrews.

Archie was a really naughty school kid.

I loved The Goon Show, we all tried to do the voices of Eccles and Bluebottle but we sounded ridiculous, we couldn't say it right like: "You dedded me."

And what about sport on the wireless, the boxing coverage was never as good as on the telly.

And then there was Luxy – Radio Luxembourg.

People thought that Luxy was just pop but it wasn't.

I remember the quizzes, Double Your Money, Take Your Pick and also Candid Microphone, well before Candid Camera, and who can forget Dan Dare Pilot of the Future?

American greats such as Bing Crosby and Doris Day had their own shows and would introduce their own hits.

There was Valentine Dyall The Man in Black. That programme would create real atmosphere. You could picture those wet streets and if there were footsteps coming up behind you, you'd think you were actually there.

There was also the American Forces Network AFN . . . Hopalong Cassidy. The radio really stretches your imagination.

JOBS AND FALSE STARTS

Some people nowadays can't talk about having any job but in our day there was no problem getting employment.

When I left the Collegiate with a couple of GCEs, I decided to be a chartered accountant because I'd heard they made a lot of money. But I ended up being a counter clerk in a plumber's merchants.

My first wage packed at Perrin and Hughes £1.17s and 6d.

After deductions it was £1.13s 4d and I gave me mam £1 2s 6d. I had ten shillings and 10 pence to last the week – and it did.

My immediate boss in the sanitary warehouse was Arthur Deacle.

He always had a fag hanging out of his mouth, always had a pair of overalls on, and was a real firm's man.

Our tearoom was a gas ring, nothing else.

Except for a wall covered up in nudes, that Arthur had pinned up.

Once you worked the ins and outs of any job you started to skive.

We had a big stack of straw in the warehouse, which was used for packing between the washbasins.

When I knew the wagons were loaded, I used to burrow into the straw for a quick half hour, I'd see Arthur walking back and forth looking for me.

But I decided to pack it in after I dozed off and only woke when a pitchfork missed my head by about an inch.

One of the drivers had come to load his wagon and just launched into the straw with the pitchfork.

An inch either way or it would have been the end of Mrs Butler's Eldest.

We also had a boss at Perrin and Hughes, Mr Crank, who made Charles Laughton look benevolent.

In his office the top half was all glass, the only way you could sneak past was on all fours.

I was desperate to get out half an hour early one day because there was an early match on and I was just crawling past his office when he opened the door.

He said: "What are you doing Butler?"

I said: "I'm just tying my shoelaces."

It was good looking back at your first job.

Some people today never have a job to look back on and that's awful.

MAMS

One thing you never see a woman doing today is cleaning their outside upstairs windows.

Me mam used to open the bedroom windows and sit on the ledge cleaning the glass while she held on to the frame.

Everyone in the street did this – but you never heard of anyone falling out,

Mams used to fight for you too, or mine certainly did for me. She did all her fighting from the front step by shouting and arguing with the mams of kids she thought had picked on me. I think she thought I needed someone to stand up for me because I had no dad.

It was me mam's step that helped turn me into a very fit schoolboy.

You knew you daren't step on it so you had to jump from the beginning of the step to land on the grid and then leap from the grid into the lobby.

Me mam used to have her own particular sayings – well at the time I thought they were her own.

Later I found that all mams said the same kind of thing: "You'll be laughing on the other side of your face," was one of the most frequent.

This always used to confuse me.

I never could work out how you could laugh using only one part of your face.

"If the wind changes you'll be stuck like that."

That's what she said whenever I pulled a face.

"God sent you to punish me," that was another common one.

When I was naughty she'd say: "You're just like your father you are."

We had a rack in our house and it fell on my grandad once and almost gave him concussion – the times I used to hear that terrible cry, "Mind the rack."

Now, I know what I am going to say now will annoy

some mams today but it's true . . . life was much harder for women.

Me mam used to put all her washing in the dolly tub and wring everything out by hand.

We didn't have washing machines in our day. Me mam also had to put all the carpets out in the yard and brush them with a stiff brush.

There was no Hoover or machine either for her.

These days, mams don't know they're born.

And mams had to deal with people like the Prudential man. He was called Gerry Corner and he would just walk straight in to the house and call out: "Are you alright Glad?"

His visits were a ritual. Me mam never used to shut the door on the men from the clubs, she always used to pay up on the nail. Me mam used to relax by playing darts.

We had a dartboard in the house and she used to play against us when she wasn't ironing but it seemed she was at the ironing board every day of the week.

Respect for your parents, that's what it was all about when we were young.

PUBS

One of the most significant things about pubs was that you really did have to be 18 to drink.

You started going the pubs once your mates had managed to get in because you had to maintain your professional status and get served too.

The first time I tried it on was at Farrell's which was in a side street off Boundary Lane.

I can remember approaching the door at least seven times and turning around desperately trying to work out the year I would have been born in if I really had been 18.

Albert Myers who told me to ask for a pint of 'Black

Family values:
My lovely Mum and
Father-in-law Eric at
my wedding to Lesley
in 1990

A blue baby:
Guess who I support?!

Mr & Mrs:
My fairytale bride

BILLY BUTLER'S CHRISTMAS PARTY
at *The Kirkby Suite.*
051-547 2666.

28th Dec. to 2nd Jan.

Starring:
DAVID ALEXANDER.
with
Tony Brutus
Julie Craig
Paul McNally
plus
Billy's Mates!

Programme 20p

A Community, Recreation and
Leisure Services Dept. of
Knowsley Borough Council
Production in Conjunction with R McCabe Entertainments.

ADMISSION FREE
TO MEMBERS WITH THIS LEAFLET

Mardi Gras
MEMBERS NOTICE
SUNDAY FEB. 8th 730 –
LATE BAR 11·30 PM

LIVING DISCO

YES AT LAST A
DISCOTEQUE THAT LIVES UP TO ITS
NAME IN DISCS AND ATMOSPHERE
FOR EVERYONE 'REGGAE, PROGRESSIVE
SOUL, THE LOT, 'PRESIDED OVER BY THE
FEARLESS, OPPONENT OF IMITATION
DISCOTEQUES' THE NON-POSING...

Billy Butler

AND
GRAB AT
THIS
SENSATIONAL
GO-GO
DANCERS

The MIDNIGHT MOVERS

WOWEE!!!
CHRIS. WHARTON

WE'VE GOT 'EM ALL
PLUS ALL THE LATEST
SOUNDS FROM ENGLAND
AND U.S.A.

"AND YOUR OWN
DISCO TOP 20

DISC.
SALES
FROM **2/6** MORE
& MORE
AS.
BEWARE
IMITATIC

ANOTHER BUTTON ADVENTURE IN SOUND

WEST COAST
FYFE PIPER
KICK THAT LITTLE
FOOT
AT THE DISCO-TEC
MR BANG BANG
MAN
SHE BLEW A
GOOD THING
BABY HELP ME
WHATS YOUR NAME
SWEET THING
TELL HER
JERK IT
CALL ON ME
BREAKOUT
DEVIL WITH BLUE
DRESS
QUITTER NEVER
WINS
DETERMINATION
SOUL TIME
HELPLESS
NOTHING ELSE TO
SAY
DANCING PARTY

Billy Butler

194 RADIO CITY

YOUR LOCAL

High Flyers:
Publication material
came in all shapes
and sizes

HOLD YOUR PLUMS

HOLD YOUR PLUMS

THE BILLY BUTLER SHOW

Wally   **Billy**

1485AM   **RADIO MERSEYSIDE**   95.8FM

Benidorm-bound:
Nice face shame about the legs.
Acting daft on holiday in 1997

Living up to my name: Serving tea for the Mayer sisters. At the Adelphi Hotel for the Victims of Violence party, 1993

A panto fan meets a scary villain: Kids love me!

Plum crowd:
The audience lapping up
Hold Your Plums, 1995

**Guitar man
without a
Tuxedo:**
You're treading
on my foot!

Echo columnists meet:
Thumbs up for me 'n' Granty

Always kidding:
And when you grow up –
I'll still be on the radio

Seeing Red:
Liverpool legend Ray Clemence
gives me the Blues

Small things arouse small minds:
Hide and seek on the radio, another broadcasting first!

Master and servant:
Relaxing at the Lord Mayor's parlour after a gruelling Hold Your Plums programme, 1995

I meet an icon from Batman: With the world's greatest impressionist Frank (the Riddler) Gorshin

Strike a pose: Winner of the 'Star Trek' William Shatner look-a-like competition, me 2010

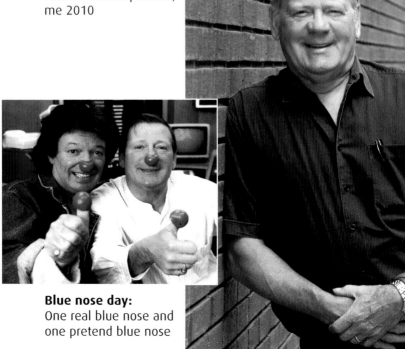

Blue nose day: One real blue nose and one pretend blue nose

Brew' led me up the path. As soon as I walked up to the barman I knew I was in a bit of trouble.

Sure enough, the first thing he said was: "Yes, son, why don't you come back when you're 18?"

When you went out drinking you could take exactly five bob with you because you knew that every pub had a fixed price for a pint.

The only time when pubs had different prices was when they had a parlour and charged you more to be served in there. They usually had a bell on the wall to ring.

It seemed more posh and was the kind of place where you went with a girl.

My regular was Emma Hughes' in West Derby Road, that was the name of the landlady. In those days if you drank in a pub all year you'd get a free pint at Christmas. Not like now when they make you pay extra.

Back behind the bar was a desert compared to now when you can get hundreds of different flavoured crisps.

Really, all you could buy was ordinary salt-flow crisps.

Occasionally, there would be a jar of pickled eggs or you could sometimes buy a plastic packet containing a triangle of cheese, a pickled onion and two dry crackers.

The pubs were frequented with characters.

There was a little fella who used to come in with a suitcase full of razor blades and toilet soap all set out in layered shelves.

I remember too, that in those days you didn't order halves, all the older men used to ask for a gill, which was the same as a half-pint measure.

I think the phenomenon today is lager. When it first came out it was a girls' drink along with Babycham, Pony, port and lemon and Cherry B's lager and lime at the time. Fellas couldn't touch it in our day.

Lager heralded the entrance into pubs of those long, posh, fluted glasses – if you want something to pose with.

Wally loved lager.

HOME COOKING

I don't think any of today's kids realise some of the delicacies they are missing out on in life.

We had stuff that they had no experience of.

I think if they did they would turn their noses up at it.

My kids used to go out in the back and cook themselves something or put a ready-made meal in the microwave.

When Mam was hard up we would get two pieces of bread, no butter on or margarine.

We didn't have butter – we only had butter on a Sunday.

ECHO margarine we used to use.

Just a piece of plain bread with nothing on and a bottle of HP sauce thickly spread on both sides and we'd go out eating it. You didn't cut it into two pieces. It did not taste as good cut into two. It had to be just the one long sandwich and it tasted glorious.

Dripping butties.

I know in our house my dripping butties always started at the bottom.

My mother used to pour the dripping into a cup and I'd always dig below the top layer of fat to get to the dark layer of fat, which had got a bit of the colour of the pan and of the beef as well.

A true dripping buttie connoisseur would tell you that dripping on hot toast was probably the crème de menthe of all dripping butties. It was wonderful.

It seemed everything came on a buttie. There would always be something in the house that you could put on a buttie. If you could not get certain luxuries there was always malt which your man would feed you to keep you healthy.

Malt was delicious spread on butties, so was marmite.

Syrup was the most damaging thing you could put on a buttie – it would pour out of the side when you bit it.

We never threw much away in our house because me

mam had already told you that there were people starving in Africa.

What I did miss – and I think it takes one of yesterday's mams to make it – is a fry up. If you left your tea the night before it never got thrown away.

Whatever was left on your dinner or your tea would all be put into one pan, and there again would be fat poured in with it and it would all be mixed around the pan until it was lovely, brown and crispy.

That would be a fry up.

I don't have fry ups now – there must have been enough cholesterol in that to kill you.

Gravy – another art form.

There was an art to making it.

Nowaways, it's just powder that you put water in.

In those days, yer mam would be out in the back kitchen for at least an hour just making the gravy, mixing the flour and putting a bit of the meat juice in.

I used to go over the road to Mrs Hatch's for my Sunday dinner just for her gravy. God bless me Mam but she was never in Mrs Hatch's Gravy League.

FLASHBACKS

If I could turn back the clock, there's one thing I'd like to do more than anything, and that's to walk down our old street, Grey Rock.

But the only way I am going to be able to do that is looking at an old copy of Kelly's Directory I got.

These detailed everybody who lived in the street.

People pay a fortune for them now.

I also looked at West Derby Road because that's where all the shops were when I was a kid. It was an adventure walking along the road then because there'd be something in every window.

I walked along one road recently and I forgot where I was – and every single shop was shuttered.

Now, when we were kids, what should have been a 10-minute walk down a road would take half an hour.

I'd love to go back to 62 Grey Rock Street and Mrs Myer's house who made toffee apples.

They were so sticky. When you took a bite they would stick to your face.

I'd like to re-visit Lee's. He had a shop at the bottom of Brunswick Road which later moved to the top of London Road. Mr Lee was the first person I know to sell American comics.

On a rainy day it'd be great to turn back the clock and sail lolly ices down a gutter. When they went down the grid it was like the Titanic going down or a German destroyer.

And I'd like to be able to go down the Pier Head and run down that tunnel or gangway that led down to it.

There was always this feeling that you were going to run straight down into the river because it was a hell of a slope.

I'd like to be able to go back and walk down those damp steps to the Cavern once again.

But there are trips down Memory Lane that you can't make if you just decide to go and do them.

For many years I wanted to walk around The Collegiate where I went to school. I should have taken the bull by the horns and asked the council – now it's too late.

I'd also love to go back to Rushworth's or NEMS and say to Mr Brian Epstein or Mr Rushworth: "Could I listen to this record please."

And you'd go to a booth and hear it.

There'd be no moans from the staff who would play as many as you wanted.

If you could turn back the clock there's so many things that you'd love to be able to do . . . just once more.

BELIEFS

Our mums would always use the bogeyman to frighten us – and we believed in him.

Childhood beliefs are great things, no-one should be without them.

I recall someone saying that every time you say you don't believe in fairies – a fairy dies. I really believed that.

I think it's a little bit sad when your own child eventually doesn't believe in Father Christmas.

It's part of their innocence gone.

When I was a kid I was convinced I'd find buried treasure. I thought the cellers and fields by us were stuffed with it – all I had to do was find a map.

Whenever I went to a library or an old bookshop I'd be convinced I'd find a map in one of the books and the treasure would be marked with a great big X.

All our gang believed it . . . I used to draw pretend maps for my mates to find and they'd be searching Newsham Park for the Spot. We used to go to Spinney Wood in Kirkby. The legend was that there was a crashed German plane there half submerged in a swamp.

You always knew a mate who'd played on it and sat in

the cockpit to say the pilot's skeleton was still there.

A lot of beliefs came from the movies.

I remember going to see The Wooden Horse in which they tunnelled out of a prison camp. My mates and me firmly believed in tunnelling then, we had plans to tunnel from our celler into the sweetshop across the road.

We really thought we'd make it – we had the wood to shore up the walls, bags to carry the stuff out in, all sorts.

We'd go looking for giants.

The daft thing was whoever was in front of you would say: "He's round the corner" and you'd leg it.

Every street had its own witch and we really believed that she cooked cats and flew on broomsticks. Whichever woman we picked on must have had terrible nightmares.

Of course the more we talked to our mates the more her power would increase. They would have a mate who she'd turned into a dog and there would always be someone who'd gone into her house never to be seen again.

And monsters . . .

I think it all came from living in an era when there were hardly any street lamps.

Films seemed a lot more frightening because you would be going from a pitch-dark environment in the cinema into a pitch-dark environment outside.

You carried your fear with you.

But one thing kids still believe in is the tooth fairy. They were a good thing as a kid, if you had regular pocket money, but if you were hard up like me they were dangerous.

I'd deliberately loosen my teeth and spend ages trying to pull them out for that penny or sometimes three pence under the pillow.

SCOUSE SAYINGS

Here begins the gospel according to me mam. Some of the things she said made no sense at all.

For instance she used to say to me: "Wait till your father comes in."

He'd left us years ago.

She would also say: "I'll go to the foot of our stairs."

What that meant I could never fathom.

Mams never ever swore, but they didn't half come out with some odd things instead, like the phrase my Gran always used to say: "Suffering ice cakes."

My mam often said: "You were sent to punish me."

I found this difficult to comprehend having been brought up as a firm believer in the stork.

"I'll wipe that smile off your face", was another, because it would have had to have been one hard belt.

And what kid has never had the words, "Do you think I'm made of money?" thrown at them.

When my mam wanted some respite from the kids she would say: "Kids should be seen and not heard."

This again used to baffle me.

Surely if we'd sat there and said nothing all the time she really would have been worried.

There's not a kid either who has not been warned:

"She's the cat's mother."

Whatever does that mean, I still don't know.

Wally remembers a threat when mams would say she was about to land you a 'go along.'

I can explain that to today's kids. It means that as you try to get away from your mam she hits you as you go along to the end of the hall.

And what about "GET IN, YOU."

Those three words were terrifying. Your mam's hand would be raised and if you got in and blamed one of your mates and said: "He made me do it," she would always say:

"If he told you to put your fingers in the fire would you do it? I suppose you would do that as well."

A favourite – there's so many of them from my mam – was: "One of these mornings you'll get up and find me gone."

Also as a last resort, mam would say: "I'm going to put you in a home."

Which was completely ridiculous, because if she had, it would have been the biggest home on God's earth – and absolutely heaving with kids.

Oh, and finally, Mrs Butler would say to her eldest:

"Billy, you're neither use nor ornament."

MOBILE PHONES

Everyone has mobile phones. i-pods, i-pads . . . all I had were shin pads (and even they were cardboard).

Now even kids in primary school have mobiles. (Mobies used to be mobile shops in my day.)

Two cocoa tins connected by a piece of string. In fact you used to shout to your mate: "Hello."

And that was the sum total of your conversation.

"Hello."

It was only: "Hello."

And then . . . "Over."

Then Dan Dare Walkie Talkies became available.

They were on string as well and again you could actually see the person you were talking to.

Even when battery-operated ones came about you could only use it for about 20ft.

Now everyone has computerised entry phones, security and intercoms.

We had a key hanging on a piece of string.

And who would have thought that one-day you cold put a square object – a video – into a machine and then the

DVD then watch your favourite film.

It definitely beats sitting on our cellar stairs with a pillow and a sheet hanging down and pulling one frame at a time through a projector.

It always amazed me that you could have the whole of the Scarlet Pimpernel in 12 frames. That was the first Hi Tech item I wanted – a projector, 9s 11d it was.

There were never any hi-tech things in our house.

These days you can make juice out of anything.

To make orange juice you needed muscles of Hercules to get a drop out of it on a glass thing.

In fact these days you can get juice out of carrots – with a liquidiser – you can get juice out of things we never thought had juice in them.

And spin dryers.

I wish they had them in my mother's day – my mam had incredible muscles on her arms because she would wring out the washing by hand.

Even toast – our toast was done by hand on the fork because it had three brown lines across the bread.

And what about football boots – they've gone high tech.

These days you put plastic studs in if it's wet.

If it's dry you put a rubber stud in.

For us it was like a general hospital operation.

We used to have a pair of pliers to get old studs off.

We would end up playing football with nails sticking through the boots.

THE DIGITAL AGE

Like me, Wally is not computer-minded. We were amazed at a computer game, like FIFA 2006, they had crowds of players doing a lap of honour, diving headers, passing – tackling and all that.

And all we had were two pipes – two goalies and a plastic ball – blow football.

In theory it was a great idea, because you had a pipe each and blew the ball to the goal at the other end.

The only snag being you ended up blowing his goalie and goal over as well.

Whoever invented blow football didn't take into account that Scousers have the biggest lungs of the lot.

There was also a 'fatality' – usually the ball which you trod on looking for it.

And the number of times I played blow football with a table tennis ball. Then, there was a tremendous advancement in football games.

We advanced to Tiddlywinks in Shoot – 10 Tiddlywinks and a goalie on a stick.

You had some great scores like 15-15 after 25 minutes.

We had some terrible fights over Subbuteo. I recall there was only one competitor to Subbuteo and that was called New Footy which was made and produced here in Liverpool.

You can get computerised cricket now with players running up bowling, batting – you name it.

Our version was called 'Owzat' with two six-sided metal rollers.

Everyone would keep score in a book.

It was two leaden weights, one with numbers one to six and Owzat!

And another featuring LBW – caught/bowled/runout/stumped/not out.

Everyone who played it cheated.

I can remember once bowling England out for 27.

There are now fighting computer games for boxing. Our boxing game had a tin ring with two boxers and you would press their heads and then throw punches and they would never hit each other.

On the lid it would say: "All the thrills of a real championship fight".

These days some computers would have 30 or 40 games

on the screen. We had compendium sets then, loads of games in a big box. You would need a cabinet from MFI to cart it around.

It's not just the advancements in TV, with cinema sound and now Plasma screens and NICAM it's like being in the pictures.

We had a 12 inch black and white screen.

Then you could send away for the ultimate – a magnifier which made the screen look 20 inches but if you sat at an angle the feller would have a 22 inch head and a 12 inch body. The sky was green and the grass blue.

These days they have computerised horse racing – what did we have?

'Escalado' where you had five metal horses and you turned a handle. A racetrack that shook and made the track vibrate so the horse could go along.

The only snag was if one fell over, the others couldn't get past it.

The horse would be lying in the middle of the course with five others lying on top of it.

On the box it said: "All the thrills of real life Horse Racing.'

And Wally and me had wooden forts.

There were some good wooden forts – especially the ones with draw bridges, which opened up thanks to a piece of cotton. Wally's fort was burned down by a mate he completely wiped out, Ford Scott, and then claimed Sitting Bull did it.

HOME

One of the things I remember most is how we had basically three rooms – the parlour, the kitchen and the back kitchen.

The parlour was for high days and holidays – it was where you were allowed to sit with your girl when you brought her home to meet your mam. The back kitchen was equivalent to the kitchen today – where all the cooking and washing was done.

And we used to live in the kitchen and gather round the table to eat all our meals.

Talking about sitting with your girlfriend in the parlour, you could sit there but there was no way you could ever get up to any hanky panky.

I could hear me mam in the kitchen rustling the ECHO and if the gaps between the numbers on the record player were too big she would always shout, "What's going on in there."

We had an awful metal statue that looked like the Statue of Liberty – a woman holding a torch.

There was a large fruit bowl on the sideboard too, but we never had any fruit in it.

I always liked me mam's kitchen drawers – they were great for rummaging around in.

Every time she found something lying about she would put it in the drawer so you could always find something interesting like ollies or string in there.

They were great for rooting around in but your mam could always tell you'd been having a ferret and used to give you a telling off.

I always had to black lead the grate – me mam always told me to do it in a way that sounded as if she was doing me a favour. We always used stuff called Zebra to do the black leading.

It was great when you got a big piece of coal to break up – the fire would really spark and flare up.

Another distinctive thing about our homes was they always had back yards – never gardens.

And in the yard there was always a dolly tub, which was kept filled with water.

Decorating around the house is one of the few things that I can do. I had quite a practice from an early age because we had no dad around. We always made paper paste from flour and water.

We never had the proper tools of the trade in our day.

I always seemed to be using nail scissors to cut the wallpaper or trying to slap flour and water paste on with a small paintbrush.

The toilet was always outside which used to present certain pitfalls – there was no light so you used to have to go into the backyard like an Olympic torch bearer carrying a rolled up ECHO that you'd put a match to.

Sometimes I used to really annoy me mam by taking a proper candle down there so I could read on the toilet.

COLLECTING

I think I started off collecting comics. They play a big part in my life.

Comic collecting in my day was a lot different than it is now. You were only a second division collector if you collected British comics.

The American comic collectors were the ones that were looked up to.

But you could only do that if you knew one of the few shops, which actually sold them.

There were two things you collected, Superman and Captain Marvel.

At the bottom of the first page it would have, "for swaps come to . . ."

And that's where you'd get your contacts.

Wally used to collect bottle tops but they weren't just milk bottle tops. Most of them were off beer bottles actually.

We used to refer to them as jinx. And they were coloured as well.

The goldmine for jinx collecting was a brewery where

you could sneak in where the broken bottles used to be and actually come away with necks of broken bottles.

The other thing I collected was ciggie packets.

Now I've never smoked at all but I can name you every cigarette brand.

So whenever we finished in the pictures we'd stay behind and look up and down the aisles for ciggy packets. You would have your Craven A, State Express or whatever.

We also collected bubble gum cards.

The ones with Mars Attack Bubble Gum even had certain numbers, which were eventually banned. Those were the ones that were really sought after.

There was one called 'Killing a Dog'. It showed a dog that had been blasted by a Martian creature. A set of those now will set you back between £500 and £900. And a wrapper itself – wow!

One of those great things about collecting was opening the packet to find just one of the five free cards you didn't have.

Then when you got together with your mates you'd find you were all missing the same one.

I don't understand why people collect car and train numbers. I still think why do they do that?

I used to put them in the same league as you'd put swots in a school.

Another thing was a lolly ice wrapper. The cinema was a great place to collect them. There were also litterbins at the bus stops. You could even collect bus tickets – that's another one.

But the Eldorado of ice cream wrapper collecting was after the Orange Lodge had been in Newsham Park.

I can remember sending wrappers off for a prize and waiting and waiting and waiting and getting a cricket bat and three stumps. And of course we all had ollies and like comics you were looked upon as a second-class citizen if you had British ollies.

They were completely clear just plain glass. We used to call them bottle washers.

The American ones were incredibly colourful. The pièce de résistance was the poly, all in white, with blood red flashes through it.

POP RECORDS

I often used to buy 78s – but they were always for other people because when I was a kid we didn't even have a record player.

One of the earliest songs I remember was called The Wedding of The Painted Doll.

I used to go over the road to Mrs Hatch's house. She and her daughter Marjorie had a load of records and they used to let me go over there and listen in.

I recall Guy Mitchell, Frankie Laine and Doris Day were on Phillips Record label.

I think most of the big recording artistes were. There was a big problem with 78s – when you played your favourite record over and over the hole in the middle got bigger and bigger and eventually the music would sound out of tune because the middle was round a spindle.

People used to have a box with all the needles in.

You were only supposed to play each one about eight times because after that they'd wreck the record. The earliest record I remember buying, cost five and seven and that included entertainment tax.

One of my most vivid memories is playing 10 records at once using the auto-changer.

This meant that you could listen to all your favourite songs in succession which you can't do today unless you put them on a cassette tape.

Everyone seemed to have a Dansette record player. And

they always seemed to be mottled in colour. Mottled white.

All they had was an 'on' and 'off' and volume – no other controls at all.

The more expensive machines might have had a treble but there never seemed to be a treble and bass.

I loved the private booths. You'd never needlessly part with your six and eight pence.

Discerning record buyers used to ask to listen to the B side as well as the A side.

You wanted two good sides for your money.

Looking back, I had two sad songs when I had the suspicion I was about to be dumped.

I played Will You Still Love Me? by The Shirelles.

When it had happened and I was feeling really sorry for myself, it was My Last Date With You by Skeeter Davis.

I'd sit in the parlour with all the lights off and feel really miserable.

Record collecting was really important to us because it was our only way of keeping in touch with the stars.

We never saw them on TV – especially the American singers.

We might have had no clear idea of what Eddie Cochran, Buddy Holly or Gene Vincent looked like but we were in absolutely no doubt about how good they all sounded.

TELLY

It's only that now we have satellite channels and cable channels that we realise most of our programmes we saw as kids were terrible.

One that comes to mind is Mark Saber . . . the one-armed detective.

A Scotland Yard Detective with a bad overcoat and one arm. And in fight scenes he would knock someone out with one punch. In those fight scenes he would inevitably end up getting someone with their arms behind their backs and yet he only had one arm himself.

When we look at it he must have been a real British hero to us – he had a square jaw.

Another series was The Grove Family. Granny Grove played by Nancy Roberts made Ena Sharples seem like Claudia Schiffer, according to Wally.

Granny moaned at everything.

Had it been a modern day soap, Granny would have ended up under the patio within weeks.

She'd say things like: "I'm starved for want of nourishment."

There was another detective called Hiram Holliday. I can picture him now knocking a gun out of a villain's hands with that umbrella.

There was Fabian of the Yard and a programme called Dial 999 with Robert Beatty – it opened with a bloke dialing 999.

Now that's what I call a dramatic opening.

There was also the man from Interpol. This was the king of the bad detectives.

DAYDREAMS

When I was Billy the Kid my ambition was always to be a cowboy.

I wanted two white guns, to wear a white hat with fringes, spurs and a big white horse.

I always fancied being a chartered accountant or a lawyer but I didn't get the qualifications.

I also wanted to be a rag and bone man.

With a horse and cart.

This was because ours always had boxfuls of toys on board and I thought it was one of the perks of the job.

Then I wanted to be a lolly-ice man – that would have been nice.

I fancied riding around on a bike with an icebox full of lollipops at the front.

There must have been hundreds of kids who wanted to be coalmen, too.

Just because you got so dirty.

Then of course we all wanted to be one of the superheroes from the TV or comics – Superman himself or Captain Marvel.

Captain Marvel was my favourite. He was just an ordinary guy.

But when he said 'Shazzam' he turned into the Marvel character and could do absolutely anything.

I tried saying 'Shazzam' to myself for years when there was no one else around, but nothing ever seemed to happen.

I also wanted to be a magician, that was another of my dreams.

I did get a Peter Pan magic box one Christmas and put on my own magic show.

I cut out invitations which said 'Magic Show at Grey Rock Street, admission two pence' and got 15 people in the audience. I wore a stick-on moustache and a black plastic coat.

I'm not saying how it went but they all asked for their money back.

My top trick involved planting a playing card in someone's pocket which I managed to do as they were all coming in, but the person found the card before they were supposed to.

And that was the highlight of my act ruined.

I also wanted to be a goalkeeper mainly because the green jerseys they wore were so brilliant.

I got one for Christmas or a birthday one year with one of those fold over roll collars.

Most of the ambitions I had seemed to have been selfish ones. For instance, I also fancied being a street cleaner because you got to open a grid with a pole and the grid was always full of ollies and money.

The same sort of treasures were there to be found if you were one of the men who cleaned out the roof guttering.

JOKE SHOPS

When you are talking about tricks and jokes you sent away for, two things spring to mind.

The Ellisdon's adverts on the back of every comic – I think the address was High Holborn in London – and the Wizard's Den in Moorfields.

I once had an Ellisdon's catalogue and I'd love to look through one again.

But there was stuff on the back of American comics that was only a dream for you. I remember an army full of 101 soldiers and cars and tanks and all sorts of things – all this in one box.

My little mind was convinced that if I got an American wireless I could listen to American programmes on it.

A lot of people remember when I was on TV with Jimmy Saville on Thank Your Lucky Stars.

I knew he'd be on that weekend with his trademark big cigar, so I went to the Wizard's Den and bought an even bigger, giant plastic cigar. You unscrewed the top and put a lit ciggie in it.

You could blow smoke out of it and people thought it was a genuine cigar.

I brought it out of my inside pocket when Jimmy came on – it's amazing how many people still remember that.

Another thing you could get was a Seebackroscope. With this you could see behind you.

But there was a great danger when you attached it to your eye if you were walking in front of a bus.

They were a deadly danger.

There were also things you put on cars to make them look as though they had been scratched – it looked nothing like it at all.

And you could buy something called Smashing Glass – this little piece of tin plate which, when you dropped it on the floor, was supposed to get your mam rushing out because she thought you'd smashed a window – it was hopeless.

There were so many simple things which could give you a laugh for just sixpence. They would give you so much amusement.

Wally pointed out to me about something that we would most certainly have sent away for – the Charles Atlas course. This was the original for seven shillings (so Wally sent off for it first).

It said: "Don't let people kick sand in your face" and it was called Dynamic Tension. It was on the back of every comic and everyone sent away for it.

I was terrified of going down the beach. I thought beaches everywhere would now be populated with fellas who would kick sand in my face.

SUNDAY PAPERS

When I was a kid, only the front page of the Liverpool ECHO was important to me, because from the top to the very bottom of that huge broadsheet page there were picture house ads.

That was all I needed to know, what was on at what

cinema. My mam and Mrs Myers would go through them and say: "Oh, listen to this lovely verse" and then they would read them out to each other.

Gradually though, I moved on from the front page cinema ads to the personal columns.

In those days it really was personal. It would be full of things like: "Sorry, couldn't be there last night. J"

Or, "C, not possible tonight – same place tomorrow 7.30pm. D"

Some of the messages ran and ran. They were like reading a soap opera.

I used to think about going down to the meeting place to see what was going on. They really intrigued me.

Aunty Joan's children's crossword was the only crossword I could ever do.

Gussie Goose and Curly Wee were the ECHO's own creations.

I found at home a 1956 children's Christmas Club card for a Curly Wee annual.

It took me from September to save up and pay for it.

In the Saturday afternoon edition of the ECHO there were two full children's pages with comic strips.

Superman, Gun Law and Wagon Train were the ones I always used to collect.

But of course, the one we all read was the Back Entry Diddlers by George Green, about a gang of scruffs who played footie.

They were absolutely brilliant.

Those ECHO supplements pre-dated the Sunday supplements they have today by years and years.

We got hours of fun out of that kids' section.

The Football ECHO was always a must.

There'd be queues standing on corners waiting for it to arrive.

Then this van would go past and a batch of footie ECHOs would fly out, there'd be a scramble to get them.

The ECHO must have had great vendors.

All the newsagents used to shut around 5.30pm back then, so the only way you could get one after that was from a street seller.

You could be in your kitchen and you'd still hear him shouting "ECHO!" down the road.

I think they must only have taken on ex-town criers.

You always lived in hope that the ECHO would make a mistake and publish a photo you already had in the Charlie Buchan Football Monthly or something.

One thing I've always wondered about is why the people who used to report the matches in those days never used their real names,

They do nowadays but then they used to call themselves things like Ranger and Scott.

One really popular columnist was George Harrison and his Over the Mersey Wall.

It was probably the most famous column ever to have appeared in the ECHO.

The first mention I ever got in the ECHO was in George Harrison's column.

It was round about 1963 and I was on Thank Your Lucky Stars. It went something like: "You may be wondering who the cheeky Scouser is appearing every week on Thank Your Lucky Stars.

"His name is Billy Butler."

Helen Shapiro was on that Saturday and he printed a picture of her instead of me.

LOCAL SHOPS

The local shop was somewhere you'd find out that someone had died.

If it happened, the corner shop would know all about it.

The thing about buying stuff in corner shops was that

quantity didn't matter. You see senior citizens today who can't afford to buy a pound of something, but the old corner shops would serve you a slice of something.

And that's how the term 'loosie' came about, because they would sell you just ONE ciggie.

All the shops gave tick and the owners had their own ways of describing customers in the book they used,

My mam was the 'blonde-haired lady with the glasses'.

The city centre had changed most of all. I always headed for Hobbies which was in Tarleton Street.

It had everything. I could look at the things in the window all afternoon.

Blackler's is a much-missed store. I didn't think of it much as a shop, more a bazaar. The department I loved most, strangely enough, was the stationery department.

It seemed to have more pens, books and writing pads than any shop in the world.

I could have spent all day in the stationery department.

Today kids have lots of sports shops but there were only two in Liverpool when I was younger – Jack Sharp's and one other, which I can't remember the name of somewhere on Old Hall Street, but it was there.

We used to get Provident and Freemans' cheques.

Me ma would say: "I've got a cheque. We'll go and get a pair of shoes."

Another shop I remember which was near us was called Lefevere and Martin, but it was known as Leafie and Martin because we couldn't pronounce it.

And another shop dearly missed is Phillips Son and Nephew in Whitechapel. If you wanted a book that's where you went. It was wonderful walking around there.

But it wasn't just the shops that were special. I can remember travelling down into town with me mates just to go on the escalators at Lewis's.

We thought they were one of the great wonders of the world.

GIRLS, WRESTLING AND ME

To impress girls I often took off on elaborate flights of fancy.

Or, to put it another way, I lied through my teeth.

Wally Scott must have had more flights of fancy in one week than I've had in my entire life!

Wally once told a girl he was Allan Clarke of The Hollies because people told him he looked like him. Whenever Wally went for meals after that, he had to say to the girl "They know me as Allan."

A girl actually wrote to me to tell me that — that's how I found out. Wally, however, was subtler than me.

I went to extremes.

I fancied this one girl who showed absolutely no interest in me, so in a desperate attempt to get her to go out with me, I told her sister I had a fatal illness. But even that didn't work.

Like anybody else, sometimes you feel you need a bit more than God gave you. So many was the time I'd been "training to be a pilot."

There was a girl called Jeanette, who I managed to charm enough to see me at least four times — which was pretty good for me in my younger days.

Mind you, that's because I told her Cliff Richard was a friend of mine.

This was enhanced when I gave her an autographed photo of Cliff – luckily, she didn't recognise my writing.

There were always the heroism tales, as well.

I've lost count of the number of people I rescued from the River Mersey. This was sometimes mixed up, to include rescuing people from burning houses and children from the fangs of dogs.

There was one girl I fancied, called Anne Hughes, whose mother used to go and have her tea leaves read by my mate's mother. I got my pal to get his ma to say to Anne's mother: "Your daughter is going to cop off with Billy Butler and they will be very happy, settle down together, make a lot of money and have a wonderful life."

But it didn't work.

Anne and I used to walk to school and imagine things, like I was pushing her from in front of a speeding car and me getting killed by the motor and saying how much I loved her before I died.

I said to one of my mates Bobby Thomas: "Next time you are talking to Anne Hughes say to her 'Do you know Billy Butler fancies you?'"

Then I was terrified to ask him what had happened in case the answer was wrong and in the end he told me what she actually said: "Oh, no, he doesn't does he . . ?"

I used to have a girlfriend called Hilda.

The one thing we both had in common was that we loved the wrestling at The Stadium.

Her idol was Jack Pye. I told her I knew his brother, Dominic, and that he'd introduced me to Jack and that Jack knew me.

This night, Jack was just coming out of the ring.

Hilda said: "Say hello to him," and so, as he walked past, I said: "Hello Jack," and he pushed me back into my seat.

I told Hilda: "He likes to crack on that he's even mean to his mates!"

Other courting days don't bring back happy memories. They were fraught.

Wally Scott was always better looking than me. I was never very confident because I always scared of girls saying "NO!"

I always seemed to have bad luck.

Nine times out of ten, if I copped off with someone and she knocked me back, my mates would bump into one of her pals and they would say to one of my pals: "My mate went out with Billy Butler on Saturday – and she said he was hopeless."

The one place to go to cop off was The Locarno.

But I had this terrible handicap: a) I couldn't dance and b) I didn't have the nerve to try.

Luckily, we were always playing football at the time so when my mates and me – Albert, Bobby and Tommy – were going to the dance I'd always get my mum to bandage my ankle. So when we got to the Locarno and the lads would say: "Let's have a dance."

I'd say: "I can't, I've hurt my ankle," and I'd pull my pants up to show them the bandage so I wouldn't have to try and dance.

The other thing you lived in fear of was when there were two girls and three fellas, so there were three of you chatting up two of them – I always knew I would be the one who didn't get a girl.

I was so unsure of myself that if I fancied someone I used to have to ask one of my mates to say – off hand – to the girl: "Billy Butler fancies you."

Getting ready to go out on the town was another problem.

My grandad had this stuff, which I would use, that was like Vaseline and your hair would end up rigid after you'd used it. The trouble was when it rained you really had problems.

You know what it's like when a candle starts dripping down a bottle . . . it was just like that.

It would come melting down my face.

M.B.E
(MY. BEST. EVERS)

*MBE stands for Mrs Butler's Eldest as
well as 'My Best Ever.'*

*Everyone likes lists.
I enjoy compiling them.*

*On air, Merseyside people are the quickest-witted
I have ever come across.
I would throw out a suggestion to listeners such as:
"Tell me 10 excuses for being caught
naked in a wardrobe."
The switchboard would be red hot.
Or: "Ten sick notes that historical figures or characters
would send in to the teacher to get the day off."
Also in this section, you will see my special Sheriff's
badge given to My Best Ever – favourite things.*

Signs You're Not Liked

- Your dad took you to the Kop and made you wear a Man United kit.
- Your dad enters you in a javelin-catching competition.
- Your ma reported you missing after four years.
- Your brother forgot your birthday – and you are TWINS.
- Elephants forget you.
- Your imaginary friend hated you.
- You tell yer ma that you are running away from home and she packs for you.
- You Played 'TICK' by yourself.
- Your shadow prayed for a dull day.
- Even Daniel O'Donnell doesn't like you.

Forgotten Saints

Patron Saints of . . .
- Doughnuts – St Dunkin
- Smokers – St Bruno
- Peeping Toms – St Luke
- Shoplifters – St Robin
- Fighters – St Barney
- Cobblers – St Lucille
- Hardup Smokers – St Lucy

Senior Citizen Hits (Golden Oldies)

- Rolling Stones – I Can't Get No Embrication
- Tom Jones – You Can Leave Your Wig On
- The Who – My Medication
- Abba – Denture Queen
- Police – Every Gasp You Take
- Bee Gees – How Can You Mend a Broken Hip
- Procol Harem – A Whiter Shade of Hair
- Roberta Flack – The First Time I Ever Forgot Your Face
- Ian Dury – Hit Me With Your Walking Stick
- Marty Wilde – A Pensioner In Love

Comedy Angels in Heaven

- Eddie Flanagan
- Jackie Hamilton
- Eddie Colinton
- Al Dean
- Sonny Jones
- Camp David
- Ted Ray
- Johnny Hackett
- George Roper

Mrs Butler's Eldest

Beatle Songs

● PLEASE PLEASE ME – Heard them first do this live at the Majestic Ballroom in Birkenhead at the Merseybeat Awards.

● THE LONG AND WINDING ROAD

● I SAW HER STANDING THERE

● HERE COMES THE SUN

● GOOD DAY SUNSHINE

● CARRY THAT WEIGHT

● PS I LOVE YOU

● I'LL GET YOU

● FOR NO ONE

● IN MY LIFE

Prehistoric TV and Radio Shows

● Randall and Hopkirk (Alive)

● Custer's First Stand

● Top of the Grunts

● Only Fools and Dinosaurs

● Play Your Slates Right

● The Lava Birds

● Silence of the Tyrannosaurus

● Around the World in 30 Minutes

● Mrs Dale's Tablets

126

Life's Mysteries

● We know the old woman who lived in a shoe but what was the name of the street?

● How does Dracula get his hair parting so straight if he can't see in a mirror?

● What does Geronimo shout when he jumps out of an aeroplane?

● Did anyone ever beat the nine-headed hydra at blow football?

● How tall was Yorik before he became a skull?

● Who washed up at the Last Supper?

● What was Quasimodo's Christian name?

● What kept Ghandi's kecks up?

● Where do all the ugly women go when you are drunk?

● Why is there an S in Lisp?

Things About life

● Children laughing

● Breathing

● Everyone laughing

● Hugging

● Kissing

MY BEST EVER

TV Westerns

● MAVERICK (1958) – This had it all, humour, action, great writing and equally great guest stars. The Maverick Brothers: James Garner (wonderful actor) as Bret; Jack Kelly as Bart; Roger Moore as Beau and Robert Colbert as Brent.
It has stood the test of time.

● THE DAKOTAS (1963) – Taken off after 17 episodes due to gratuitous violence. The fabulous Jack Elam started as J D Smith – brilliantly menacing.

● ALIAS SMITH AND JONES (1971) – Another series with humour as its base and more great stories. Thaddeus Smith and Joshua Jones alias Ben Murphy and Pete Duel. Sadly, Pete committed suicide in December 1971 during the series and Roger Davis who actually narrated the opening titles replaced him.

● CENTENNIAL (1978) – An epic of mammoth proportions over 20 hours. Start watching and you are hooked. Western brilliance of triumph and tragedy.

● LONESOME DOVE (1994) – Almost equalled the above for a great performance by Tommy Lee Jones as Woodrow F Call.

● DEAD MAN'S GUN (1977) – Great series following the adventures of a cursed revolver and the people who used it in the old West. Produced by . . . Henry Winkler.

● LAWMAN (1958) – John Russell as Marshall Dan Troop.

I can still pull 'em: Me with Edith Bramley on her 100th birthday. Presenting her with an alarm system as part of the Sefton Help's Aged Alarm appeal

Great ambassadors: Mersey cats at a special Variety Club lunch at The Grafton, with Irene Oram, head-teacher of Foxfield School, 1993

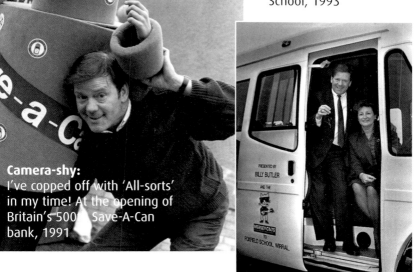

Camera-shy: I've copped off with 'All-sorts' in my time! At the opening of Britain's 500th Save-A-Can bank, 1991

Mersey pride:
Stan and I look well, but what's with the long face Wally?
Radio history made when a talking donkey appeared 'live' on my show, 1990

Out of his skull:
With our mate Yorik at his book signing, along with the writers Andrew and Bernard Galbraith, 1980

Fax appeal:
With Bill Oddie and
Debbie Rix. Publicity
photo for Fax TV series

Contractually yours:
'Thank Your Lucky
Stars' approach me to
appear the show in
1962

Mr. Butler,

We would like you to appear on the Spin-A-Disc
l again in Thank Your Lucky Stars on Sunday 18th February,1962
lpha Television Studios, Aston Road North, Birmingham 6.

Would you please telephone me (reversing the charge)
week, and let me know if you are able to appear, and we can
irm the time and your travel arrangements. If you can manage
atch the same trains as last time this should be about right.
Telephone number is TEDdington Lock 3252 - Ext. 459 or 351.
e we shall see you again on the 18th.

Yours sincerely,

Valerie Brayden
Production Assistant

Dear Billy,

Controller, Local Radio has asked me to tell you that
you have been granted a Special Award with effect from
1st October. Your new salary is shown on the attached form
and you will be eligible for annual increments up to your
new special roof of £5454. The special roof exceeds the
normal roof of the grade by the amount of the Special Award.
Your incremental date remains unchanged.

This Special Award has been given to you because of the
sustained outstanding merit of your work. It is additional
to the annual increment which can be earned and represents
a continuing addition to normal salary so long as you remain
on your present grade and your work continues to show
outstanding merit.

Yours sincerely,

(Robin Bather)
Senior Personnel and
Administrative Officer, Local Radio

Praise from above:
Granted the
Special Award'
or my commitment
o the show

Cartoon capers:
How cartoonist
Pete King
depicts
Billy and Wally,
1995

Plum machine:
The enigmatic 'Edgar'

On Air:
My Jordan impression.
At Radio Merseyside
in 1995

Getting a lift home:
Winner of worst sweater of the year award.
At Whitechapel Chippie, 1987

By Royal Appointment:
The Queen is not impressed
with my t-shirt, 1996

Tuxedo time: A band reunion with Billy Kinsley and Alan Crowley at a Variety Club tribute

Handy man?: Lesley has nailed again with her b on my DIY disast

WANTED, £2 Re
Me and Terry A▮
chairman of the
Tombstone Cou▮
Music Club – rai▮
money for the ▮
Autistic Society,
April 2010

0
3
9
3
5
2
2

LONDON
07.12.06
SW1

Billy Butler MBE
Radio Merseyside
55 Paradise Street
Liverpool L1 3BP

Honoured Indeed:
Tony Blair really thinks
I'm an MBE!

Now he really looked like a Lawman – and the series had some great guest stars. Though his deputy played by Johnny McKay was a nuisance.

● ADVENTURES OF BRISCOE COUNTY JUNIOR (1993) – Western series with added Sci-fi. An 80s 'Wild Wild West'. Lead role played brilliantly by Bruce Campbell who was noted for his horror role in Evil Dead.

● THE LONE RANGER (1949) – Most stirring music of all. Tonto, played by Jay Silverheels, always got battered. I could never work out how Clayton Moore got in those trousers. There's a hilarious skit on the Billy Cosby album about the Lone Ranger.

● DEADWOOD (2004) – My word . . . I never realised cowboys cussed like that. Ian McShane made a great villain.

Failed Careers

- Taxman – Ken Dodd
- Midget – Peter Crouch
- Avon rep – Quasimodo
- Corpse – Lazarus
- Stand-up comic – Yorik
- Heckler – Marcel Marceau
- New Year Letter-Inner – Jonah
- Hide and seek champion – Mr Magoo
- Undertaker – The Laughing Policeman

Signs You Live In A Rough Neighbourhood

- You go to a Liverpool FC fancy dress party as Alex Ferguson.
- The bailiffs move you IN . . .
- Carol singers wear boxing gloves
- The mobile shop is on four bricks
- Dogs wear gum shields
- Lollipop men and ladies charge kids to cross the road
- The sun refuses to come out
- You clear your ears with a Black and Decker drill
- Wigs are nailed on
- You kiss the mother-in-law . . . on the lips

Local Artists

- The Pearl
- Amsterdam
- Pete Wylie
- Susan Hedges
- Ian McNabb
- Melissa Hart
- The Coral
- Gary Murphy
- The Zutons

US Destinations

- Scottsdale, Arizona – Absolutely beautiful cacti and mountains. Only 30 minutes from the airport. Great shops, restaurants and bars. History everywhere, just right for a drive to Tombstone or Route 66 – sunrises and sunsets just magnificent.

- Costa Mesa, California – 50 minutes from LA, great town, fantastic shopping and malls. Short drive to all the well-known beaches such as Venice Beach, La Jola etc – and the manager of the Hilton Hotel is a Scouser.

- Bandera, Texas – Just outside of San Antonio and known as 'The Cowboy Capital'. Just one main street full of bars and restaurants. Packed with tall guys with slim waists, broad chests and cowboy hats. Visit The Alamo, San Antonio and the river.

- Fort Lauderdale, Florida – Just a five-hour drive from Orlando and well worth a visit. Beautiful beaches, great entertainment venues and a fantastic flea market.

- Hawaii – Utter paradise visually with Pearl Harbour an astounding walk in history.

Tear Jerkers

● The Champ – Either the original or the remake when the child cries out "CHAMP – wake up Champ!" Your heart breaks for him. Incredible acting.

● Bridges of Madison County – A hauntingly beautiful tale of a secret love affair revealed after death. Superbly acted by Clint Eastwood and Meryl Streep. The soundtrack is beautiful, too.

● Always – Such an undervalued Spielberg movie in which Richard Dreyfus returns to earth after his death as a guardian angel but finds it hard to cope watching the girl he loves being pursued by another man. He eventually has to go into her head to tell her to stop loving him. How can you do that?

● Forrest Gump – Tenderly emotional. Forrest's undying love for Jenny – no matter what the cost – is superb, as is the scene where she tells Forrest the child is his and the scene where Forrest talks at her graveside, well, endless tissues needed.

● The Notebook – Emotionally heart-warming, James Garner again showing what a brilliant actor he is.

Wishes

You've got one wish – here are some . . .

- Wee Willie Harris – I wish I could change my name
- William Tell's son – I wish it was a pumpkin
- Sampson – I wish I'd just had a neckshave
- Ghandi – wish I had a zip fly
- Goliath – I wish people wouldn't throw stones
- Moses – I wish I'd had a writing pad
- Bill Bailey – I wish I'd gone home
- Abraham Lincoln – I wish we would have had a TV
- Michaelangelo – I wish I'd had a paint roller
- Headless Horseman – I wish I'd seen that low bridge
- The Eunuch – You know what I wish!!!

Signs of the Times

- You go online to chat to a person you have never met in a country thousands of miles away and yet you haven't spoken to your next door neighbour for months
- You try to enter a password into the microwave
- You try to change TV channels with your mobile phone
- You email your son upstairs to tell him dinner's ready
- He emails you back to ask you "What is it?"

Life's Puzzles

- Who was the bogeyman frightened of when he was a child?

- How did the Phantom of the Opera get a piano down the manhole?

- What did the first man who milked a cow think he was doing?

- Who taught the three bears how to make porridge?

- Did the Mummy put a claim in?

- Who did the first person to catch a cold catch it off?

- Why don't they sell mouse-flavoured food for cats?

- What happens to an 18 hour girdle after 18 hours?

- What was the best thing before sliced bread?

Signs to give up Footy

- You're the only one in the free kick wall with your hands by your side

- You put glasses on to take a penalty

- You leave your undies on in the shower

- You accuse the corner flag of pulling tongues at you

- You can't remember which way you are kicking

- You try to cross a balloon

134

- The ref asks for next of kin
- You get stretchered on
- Your pension book is stolen from the dressing room

Failing Eyesight Clues

- You try to change TV channels with a bar of fruit and nut
- You warm your hands in front of the telly
- You go to the Grafton and take your wife home!
- You go to Anne Summers and ask for a bag of chips
- You say to Jordan, "Hello Tom"
- You can't find Liverpool ONE
- You offer a fur coat a bone
- You try to carve the tea cosy at Sunday lunch

Useless Presents for Famous People

- Yorik – Stilts
- The Mummy – A monocle
- Headless Horseman – A trumpet
- Venus De Milo – An ironing board
- Dracula – A mirror

- Uncle Fester – Brylcream
- Ghandi – A snake belt
- Man in the Iron Mask – Aftershave
- Captain Hook – A condom
- Olive Oyl – A push-up bra
- Vanessa Feltz – A hoola-hoop
- Adam and Eve – Washing machines

Responses to Being Found Naked in a Wardrobe

- "Is this where the Ghandi look-a-like contest is taking place?"
- "Who's moved my Superman outfit?"
- "Has your wife counted all the way to 20 already?"
- "Hello – I was just trying your flares on."
- "Is this lift going down?"
- "That was some stag night . . ."
- "Yer sauna's not working."
- "Don't suppose you've got a Hamlet on you, have yer?"
- "I'm just finishing your shower cubicle off."

Daft Questions to Obvious Situations
(Bet you've been asked them!)

- You are pushing your car down the street and someone says: "Won't it start?"

- You stagger in with two loaded Asda bags and he says: "Have you been shopping?"

- You put your coat on and she asks: "Are you going out?"

- You go to the barbers and he says: "Haircut Sir?"

- You come in soaking wet and she says: "Is it raining?"

Unforgettables

- Transfers – Great big sheets of incredibly multi-coloured things. Usually 24 to a sheet. Disney characters/flags, etc. There is always the mystery of whether you wet the back of your hand first and then put it on or whether you put it on and then wet the back of the transfer.

- Stilts – We used to play on stilts, walking around on these long poles with a step half way up.
Kids who couldn't afford them, or whose dads couldn't make them, used to have milk tins or empty tins of any-thing, and put string through them that went up and over their shoulders to walk around in them.

● Gutters – Sail paper ships down them . . . great places for imagination for young pirates.

● Darned socks – I always used to have my socks darned. The heel . . . it was always the heel.

● Patched trousers – Talking of wool. You never see kids nowadays with patches on their trousers. We're that well-off these days that you can afford to get new kecks. Many's the time I've been to school with a grey pair of trousers with a black patch on.

● Plastic tablecloths – They were always either red check or blue check and full of ciggie holes. One tablecloth woud last you for years. All you had to do was rub it with a wet cloth.

My Best Ever — Sick Notes for Famous People

● Mrs Yorik – "Our Yorik won't be in today, he's got athletes forehead."

● Jonah's Mam – "Our Jonah can't come into school today, he was run over by the school bus."

● Simple Simon's Mum – "Simon won't be coming in today he's ill. PS I wont be in tomorrow, either."

● Mrs Noah – "Please excuse Noah he won't be in today – He's got distemper, rabies, myxomatosis, bird flu and foot and mouth disease."

- Mrs Joshua – "Our Josh won't be in today, he was practicing his trumpet and a wall fell on him."

- Mrs Dracula – "Our Drac can only go to night school."

- Mrs Olive Oyl – "Poor Olive won't be in today, she's got a bad chest."

- Mrs Lecter – "Our Hannibal won't be in today, he ate someone who disagreed with him."

- Mrs Lazarus – "Our Laz won't be in. He's Dead. He'll be in tomorrow."

 **Nothing Nicer Than . . .**

- The smell of a new born baby
- That first kiss
- Being in love
- Laughing till your sides ache
- Your Mam combing your hair
- Getting in a hot soapy bath
- Having your back scratched
- Someone you love saying I love you back

Famous Higson's Beermats: List of Scouse Characters

- Pierre Head
- Albert Dock
- Penny Lane
- Doc Road
- Rock Ferry
- Lord Street
- Gladwys Street
- Anne Field
- Victoria Monument
- Stanley Park
- Phil O'Monic
- Clayton Square
- Otto Spool
- Kirk Dale
- Count Erode
- Birk'n'Head
- Olive Mount
- Norris Green
- Liz Card
- Ma Gull

Famous Liverpudlians

● Dixie Dean – legend. There's a statue showing the importance of the man.

● Davey Hickson. He was all a centre forward should be. He was the kind of centre forward you read about in the Wizard, the Rover and the Hotspur. He always seemed to be going forward, whereas today's footballers go sideways.

● Alan Bleasdale. I admire him as a writer and as a person as well – he's a very honest and very funny man although he's got one of the gloomiest outlooks on life I've ever known! He's a fabulous bloke.

● Willy Russell. The great thing about him is he is so approachable.

● I've worked with Ken Dodd all my life. What makes him special? I think it's his relentlessness! He just keeps going and going and going. Today, we have very funny stand ups like Steve Gribbin, Sam Avery and Keith Carter.

● Billy Fury was a good person. I interviewed him once or twice and he was one of my early idols. He was probably the only genuine British rock and roller that we've ever had – he was streets ahead of everybody else and the nearest thing we ever had to Elvis Presley.

● Frankie Vaughan was another wonderful person and someone who was emotionally moved quicker than anyone I've ever known. He would fill up at the slightest mention of where he grew up or if he received praise or anything like that.

● Rex Makin – A brilliant solicitor and a clever man. Plus, he's more warm-hearted than he'd like you to know

 **Unlikely Jobs for Famous People**

● Ulrika Johnson – Marriage counsellor

● Long John Silver – Line dancer

● The Hunchback of Notre Dame – Ceiling paperer

● Ghandi – Speedo model

● Cyclops – Binocular salesman

● Phantom of the Opera – Lift attendant

● Rev Ian Paisley – Snooker commentator

● Nine-headed Hydra – Film extra

● Little Bo Peep – Security guard

● Frankenstein – Avon rep

Surnames to Avoid

- Mr and Mrs Seville – Barbara
- Mr and Mrs Kerr – Nick
- Mr and Mrs Bare – Tim
- Mr and Mrs Bum – Ophelia
- Mr and Mrs Curry – Henrietta
- Mr and Mrs Tarse – Ty
- Mr and Mrs Gunn – Tommy
- Mr and Mrs Nimmo – Don
- Mr and Mrs Legg – Peg
- Mr and Mrs Oslea – Rick
- Mr and Mrs Curtain – Annette

Unmade TV Series

- It Ain't Half Hot Mum, starring Joan of Arc
- Donald Duck – The Bill
- Rudolph Hess – Neighbours
- Beethoven – Name that Tune
- Dracula – Good Morning
- Invisible Man – You've been Framed
- The Pope – Men Behaving Badly

- Vanessa Feltz – Bottom
- Yorik – Casualty
- Salmon Rushdie – Surprise Surprise

 **Places to Take People in Liverpool**

- The Beatles' Story exhibition, which has recreated the Cavern to a remarkable degree. If I could tell you what the atmosphere was like when I worked there, lunchtimes and evenings six days a week! I was with the Tuxedos and we played the Cavern 12 or 13 times, including one mammoth night when we topped the bill . . . which turned out to be the same night as The Beatles had their welcome home at the town hall, so it was probably the smallest attendance the Cavern's ever had. I'd say you never really saw The Beatles unless you saw them at the Cavern.

- A tour of where the old clubs were, like the Mardi and the Downbeat – and you'd have to take people to the Blue Angel and the Jacaranda.

- Merseyside Maritime Museum, our rich heritage. Today, there are so many more places to take people, when I was young it was the Walker Art Gallery, and that was it.

- Looking forward to the Museum of Liverpool.

● The Slaughterhouse on Fenwick Street, which has comedy downstairs at the weekends – the great thing about Liverpool now is that you can take people out on a Friday or Saturday and see seven different comics. Liverpool is famous for laughter, there's nothing better than laughter! There are so many comedy venues in the city now, which is good to see.

● I also like the Cornmarket Pub, opposite the Slaughterhouse – it's absolutely brilliant and a magnificent example of great pub decor.

● The nearby Pig and Whistle on Chapel Street. It used to be the place to go for sausages, eggs and suit lengths (as well as drink)! It was a combination of a pub and a supermarket!

● Goodison Park. I think I'd start where I used to live at Grey Rock Street and walk to the match to give them my 1950s experience.

Sweets

● Boiled sweets – Leave them in your pocket for an hour and you'd need a crow bar to separate them.

● Face-pullers. The number one sweet was the Acid Drop.

● Cream Soda – Green on one side and white on the other.

● Spearmint – Wally said it was the forerunner of Superglue

- Barley Sugar Stick – 12 inches long length meant value to us.

- Lucky Dips and Lucky Bags. Wally always used to get an Unlucky bag.

- Liquorice not to be confused with Spannish. Liquorice three inches high and ¼ inch thick. I don't know why but your mouth would go completely jet black.

- Sticky Lice – Like eating a branch of a tree.

- Palm Toffee – It never broke into little pieces.

- Gobstoppers – Wally would pass on his to his mate to take over. It would be called unhygienic now.

- Chewy – I am convinced my bald patch was caused by chewing gum. I would stick it to the bed post at night, I'd wake up in the morning with a big chunk of chewy stuck to my head and my mam would cut it out with scissors.

Radio People

MY BEST EVER

- Kenny Everett
- Terry Wogan
- Jimmy Saville
- Emperor Rosco
- Chris Evans

Favourite Records by Local Acts

● The Meyer Sisters – Rain on the windows
From early 1975 written by the late John Bryant.
The nearest thing I ever heard to a late 1950's girl group.
Total anguish.

● Vicki Brown – Look for me in Rainbows
Sung from the heart by Joe Brown's late wife, who knew she was dying from cancer when she recorded it. It has brought so much comfort to so many people.

● Kenny Johnson – Today
The ultimate wedding song by our most talented country singer.

● The Pearl – Your Sweet Grace
This band made some wonderful recordings but the harmonica-led opening and the hypnotic join-in end chorus are perfection.

● Melissa Hart – Mothers' Angels
Another enormous listeners' favourite and one that has brought such comfort. If it really ended this way we would have nothing to fear. Fabulous vocals and production.

● Up and Running – Boom
A great pop record by Phil and Alex. Would have loved to see a video of it with pyrotechnics. One of the best ever local bands and Phil Jones one of our most respected singer-songwriters.

● Anthony John Clarke – That afternoon in august
Another talented singer songwriter, able to combine humour and emotion. This song is a wonderful tribute to the fallen.

● Louise Rogan – Trying to Love You
This little lady was performing for Wally and I in cabaret shows when she was 14! Now a mature and very talented artist she made this wonderful Beth Neilson Chapman song her own.

● Jeggsy Dodd – Liverpool (so good they named it twice)
A biting, funny, sarcastic tribute to Liverpool recorded for capital of culture year. Six minutes of perfection.

● Leo Dove – Liverpool
From the early 70s, one of the first homages to our fair city. Wistful and reflective.

● Amsterdam – Home
Ian Prowse is a talented lad and the record makes you feel like it says on the label!

● Pete Wyllie – Blitzkrieg Bop
Liverpool's enfant terrible. This version of the Ramones' classic is 2 minutes of punk perfection.

● Danny Roman – Turning Back the Hands of Time
Wouldn't we all like to do that? Danny sings this version of Nessun Dorma with Neil Sedaka lyrics beautifully.

Do I ever switch off?
Here's an insight

PEOPLE ask me what do I do when I am off air? Well, before the weather and traffic reports . . . here are my answers.

Q: What time do you lie in until?
A: I don't. There's too much to do in life such as going to flea markets. I would say that 9am is the latest I've slept in to. I am up as early as 7am on Sundays. I love browsing in bookshops, new and second-hand, and collectors' shops.

Q: Is there anyone famous you'd like to spend a day with?
A: Jack Palance. I'd like to be seen with him, especially in a bar. As customers came in he would say: "Who are you looking at?"

Q: Do you still go the match?
A: I've been a Blues fan since I was about eight, so that's about 60 years now. I used to be a season ticket holder. I realised it wasn't that fair on the family because, working on radio, Saturdays were my only day off.

Q: What would you pack in a picnic basket?
A: Buffalo chicken wings – hot and spicy. I love them when I'm in America. I once ate 36 of them, a brand called Vesuvius, for obvious reasons. I'd also put in a bottle of Zinfandel, Rose wine.

Q: What is your favourite Saturday night out?
A: A restaurant – and the emptier the better.

Q: Is there a programme, series or movie you would stay in for?
A: I love Father Ted, Trigger Happy TV, League of Gentlemen, My Name is Earl and Flight of the Conchords. Comedy is my bag.

Q: Do you have breakfast in bed on a Sunday – if so is it a fry-up or something healthier?
A: Sometimes a fry-up, when Les is in a very good mood. But a favourite Sunday breakfast would be a hot sausage butty at a car boot sale stall.

Q: Have you ever spent a Sunday doing DIY – we know how bad you are at it, your wife wrote a book about you.
A: No. Les won't allow me. She knows about my DIY nightmares.

Q: Do you go to church?
A: The last time was Christmas Eve a few years ago and it got me thinking. I just got out of the habit, which, I'm afraid, is the case for a lot of people.

Q: How would you spend your weekends as a child?
A: My lasting memory is mam making me wear Sunday Best. You couldn't do anything in that. You couldn't climb or go in gardens. You could, however, laugh at your mates, who were dressed in THEIR best gear.

Q: Do you exercise at weekends?
A: Les and I go for what we call 'power walks', along various proms.

Q: Would winning the Lottery change you?
A: No. I've never bought a ticket. I will when they give the money to deserving causes – and I don't mean museums. It is the peoples' money, after all.

HOLD YOUR PLUMS!

He or she who dares wins

PEOPLE say what was it like doing Hold Your Plums.

In 1991 we invited a journalist to be a fly on the wall.

Phil Key, the arts editor of the Liverpool Daily Post – Penge-born but we forgave him – went in the studio to watch us at work and see how the show went out.

This is his fly-on-the-wall account of the programme.

Phil's never been the same since seeing Maestro Butler at work – this is his story . . .

SHORTLY before 11am, presenter Billy Butler arrived at his Radio Merseyside studios in a high state of excitement.

He called over his producer Wally Scott and with an air of triumph, removed an enormous pair of underpants from a plastic bag.

"Look what I have got for the prize!" he exclaimed.

Across the front of the garment was written the slogan: "I bet he drinks Carling Black Label."

Scott giggled, before explaining that he already had two major prizes for the phone-in quiz show that day, two male posing pouches in different sizes.

Amazingly, these crude items of male apparel were to be the star (and only) prize in the radio station's biggest audience puller in its history, Hold Your Plums.

Such has been the show's triumph that congratulatory letters have come from across the world and other stations have tried similar ideas with varying success.

But, in a variation from the accustomed format, Hold Your Plums works on the premise that its contestants are basically thick.

Few seem able to answer the simplest of questions.

"Give us a clue, Billy," has now passed into radio folklore, as Butler struggles bravely to offer allegedly helpful suggestions to his baffled game-payers.

It is these moments that listeners like best – often ladled with innuendo – and have produced best-selling cassette tapes and now CDs. In one classic instance, it took a highly frustrated woman 40 minutes to come up with the name of the German football club Borussia Moenchengladbach.

A soldier in the Gulf wrote to the station to reveal that he listened to the tapes while under fire: "If you've got to go you might as well go laughing," he explained.

Although Butler and Scott work as a double act on air, they each have specific roles.

Billy as host, Scott as producer and the man who dreams up all the questions.

These are all written on a large sheet of paper, the answers held up by Scott for the live audience which forms part of the show "in case you are just as thick," Scott smiles.

Around 50 crammed into the studio, herded by the volunteers who work with the station.

One of them, Bill Townley, explained to the assembled crowd: "Remember, our callers are not stupid – they know how to dial." Scott described them as "normal people with z-levels."

With the show's reputation for bawdy humour, however, he was unnerved to spot the arrival of the Mayor of Wirral who had been visiting the station on another matter and asked to sit in the audience.

He took his place in full regalia on the front row.

Scott asked the woman next to him not to touch his knee while Butler told her: "If he touches your knee ring the newsdesk immediately."

The Mayor grinned broadly. Butler says he has an instinctive knowledge of how far to go with people.

The duo sat at a round table with a metal box described as Edgar, a so-called acronym for Electronic Digital Games Apparatus for Radio.

This object, with buttons and lights, delivered the fruit machine symbols in an electronic voice.

Although only there in a reporting capacity, having criticised the show several times in the past for its basic humour, Butler insisted that I take a role.

This was, much to my chagrin and shame, to sit at the table and act as 'nudger-watcher.'

If a contestant had three different symbols, I had to shout: "Your nudger's out!" This, I was informed, was a tremendous honour.

Happily, I had to undergo this 'honour' only once.

The tone of the show was quickly set by the first contestant, a woman named Margaret, who said that she had been up since 5.45 am because she needed to visit the toilet: "I was bursting," she added by way of explanation.

Her question concerned the method employed by King James I to show displeasure, the answer – according to the paper held up by an amused Scot – being: "Show his bum."

To everyone's amazement and the relief of Butler who thinks up his clues on the spot, the woman immediately answered: "Drop his trousers."

Informed that her possible prize was a posing pouch, she suggested that wearing one would be a problem "if you got a touch of the runs."

It was not to be her problem, Edgar failing to deliver three of the same symbols. "You've won nudden," declared Butler, the man who dreamed up the radio show after changing the radio stations and requiring a replacement for a successful quiz he had left behind.

He admits that the station bosses weren't too keen on the title.

"They told me that if the Radio Times printed it, then they would use it." Later Scott joined him and the show really took off.

Cheeky suggestiveness is one of its keys to success.

One caller, who explained that she met her husband at Moreton, was immediately asked by Butler: "Were you cockling at the time?" And Scott, who likes to push the crude comedy to the limit, added: "Did he ask to see your cockles?"

The audience roared as they did when another caller talked of castrating her pets.

Surprisingly, the show works without the aid of the regulation panic button giving a recording delay.

Engineer Peter Heneghan said it was easy to cut people off straight away if matters ever did get out of hand.

But equally popular are the dimbats, a prize offering being a woman who was unable to name the boat featured in the film Mutiny on the Bounty.

"It could have been launched by a coconut," suggested Butler to little response. The same woman had problems when asked the name of the ape in the Tarzan films.

"Monkey?" she ventured.

The show attracts listeners from a wide area, contestants from North Wales and Lancashire being among the willing participants on this two-hour broadcast.

Butler even tells of the time he was passed through Kennedy Airport by an American customs man who demanded in return a dedication on Hold Your Plums.

He had heard it on a British visit.

Unlike Scott, who has a lot of preparatory work on the questions, Butler admits that he does little in the way of rehearsal.

None, in fact.

He does not know the questions before he arrives, or who contestants will be.

"And I never get nervous before a show – not after all these years," he says.

It is the very naturalness of the presentation which, he thinks, makes it work.

"Others have tried it, but if it isn't natural, if you are working to a strict formula, then something is missing."

With the show over, both he and Scott sign photographs for delighted fans in the audience.

"Wonderful, great fun, marvellous!" the fans tell them on the way out.

The single prize of underwear is meanwhile being parcelled up for the woman who was successful in a draw of the two people who had three symbols the same.

"They always pick up the prize, no matter how terrible they are" says Scott . . .

REQUESTS
(HE'S HAD A FEW)

Billy Butler has played thousands upon thousands of requests and dedications for his listeners.

So now we turn the turntables on him.

Here are requests from friends, colleagues and celebs Read all about what fans from all walks of life think about Mrs Butler's Eldest . . . just for the record.

ALLAN WILLIAMS
THE MAN WHO GAVE THE BEATLES AWAY

Billy is a true supporter of new talent and he never sits on the fence.

He is someone I am glad to see when he walks in the room.

At my 80th birthday party more people wanted to speak to him than me. I didn't mind. He is someone you can call a friend and who believes passionately in what he does.

I know Bob Wooler would second this – (looking up to Heaven) wouldn't you, Bob?

IAN PROWSE
MUSICIAN/AMSTERDAM

There have been plenty of great DJs from Liverpool over the years but only one has become a complete institution within the city itself. All Merseyside generations are familiar with Billy Butler, the alliteration has been with us for decades now. I remember listening to him as a boy and if Liverpool is 'In England but not of it' then Billy has played a big part in that Scouse exceptionalism.

On a personal level, Billy Butler has been immensely supportive of all my records, both with Pele and now with Amsterdam. It's not unusual for him to turn up to shows and have a great night out with us either. Maybe Billy's name never got as trendy as John Peel's but his unswerving support for local bands has been completely invaluable to the Merseyside scene. Mine included.

Having appeared on his shows hundreds of times I can tell you he's a very funny man, for me the essence of him are the mad things he says to you just as you're about to go on air. Many's the time I haven't been able to speak when the red light goes on, because he's just cracked me up.

God bless ya Billy.

SPENCER LEIGH
BROADCASTER AND AUTHOR

There are many things I admire about Billy Butler – his commitment to Merseyside, his dedication to making good radio programmes, his passion for playing records that mean a lot to him, the brightness of his wit and the boldness of his questioning, often cushioned with humour.

What other interviewer would have said on air to Garry Christian, "You've got to start getting on with people"?

One of the key factors in Hold Your Plums was the way he handled contestants.

He knew how to make it worse for these poor souls and how to make them thoroughly confused without humiliating them, so that he himself could go mad with frustration.

It was a class act, probably politically incorrect by today's standards, but great for the times.

Amidst all the knockabout humour, there is a very fine wit at work.

When the Tall Ships came to Liverpool in 1984, Billy Butler mentioned on air that he had been talking to Joe Butler, the country music presenter for Radio City.

"Joe wasn't impressed," said Billy, "but then he remembers the Armada."

That was spontaneous, it was brilliant, and if Woody Allen had said it, it would have become one of the classic jokes of the last century.

My wife, Anne, also would like to pay tribute to Billy.

They are both lovers of westerns and he often lends her the films he has been watching.

They could both appear on Mastermind with 'Lonesome Dove' as their specialist subject.

'CARING STEVE' COLEMAN
BBC PRODUCER

I've worked as producer for Billy Butler, for about three years, but like many others, I feel like I've known him for much longer.

I'd be lying if I said my total excitement, when I found out I was getting my big chance working with Mrs Butler's Eldest, wasn't tainted with fear and panic!

This was Billy Butler, Hold your Plums, Billy and Wally, Mersey Pirate, Cavern DJ, not to mention a man who has met, interviewed or become friends with just about every famous person I care to mention.

Initially, working with Billy wasn't easy, not because he's difficult or anything, just because his knowledge of radio, its listeners, music and his memory of just about every film and song and showbiz celebrity can leave you feeling dizzy and lost, and I did wonder if he thought: "Who's this guy?"

One of Billy's greatest strengths though, is his ability to take you along the most amazing journey using his experience and craft of radio. He's never made me feel anything other than part of the ride.

He can spot your strengths and use them, and he knows how to take your weaknesses and make them funny.

I think it was at least 8-12 months before my mind was sharp enough to get in tune with Billy's quick and ruthless wit, although there are still plenty of times when I can see his eyes rolling in dismay at me missing the gag!

Billy can also be the biggest wind up merchant I know, on or off the airwaves. He regularly enjoys watching my face turn grey when he mentions cabaret act 'The Cunning Stunts' or the classic 'R Sole' sketch from Hold Your Plums, in the middle of the afternoon show.

The key is, despite my worried brow, he knows it makes

me smile and he knows everyone tuned in is loving every minute of it, that's just a small part of what makes Billy the legend I really believe he is.

Well, I might change my mind if he gets the pronunciation wrong and gets us both the sack!

Outside the radio station, Billy's sense of direction is quite possibly the worst of anyone I've ever known.

He must have been to the St Helens Theatre Royal loads during its existence, yet it will still take a member of the public to recognise his confusion at a petrol station and offer to take him there – Mr X you know who you are!

He must also hold the land speed record for any mammal on two legs.

He's over twenty years my elder and there's just no keeping up with him when there's good soup and papers to be read over lunch!

There simply isn't enough time or words to describe my admiration for Mrs Butler's Eldest. He's warm, fun, clever, funny, passionate and a real professional who does everything with his whole heart.

He will probably also hate all this fuss and praise, he never takes it.

I hope it continues for many years yet, I'm learning from the best and still have to pinch myself to make sure its all actually happened, but more than that, I'd like to think he's my friend.

He'll read this and think one thing of course.

What a bloody creep!

ROB FENNAH
MUSICIAN AND PLAYWRIGHT

Most recording artists remember the first time they heard their song being played on the radio.

I certainly do – I was digging up a crop of rotting sprouts within the walled gardens of Upton Convent School for Girls, having taken a job there as apprentice groundsman.

I was in a band called Buster and had decided to earn a few quid whilst waiting for two of my fellow band members to leave school.

A few months earlier we had signed a major deal with RCA Records and had already recorded our debut single, 'Sunday'. A promotional copy had been sent to Radio Merseyside's Billy Butler – a DJ renowned for helping promote local talent – so there was a fair chance he'd give it a spin.

Standing knee-deep in stinking mud, I switched on my portable radio, wrapped a scarf over my face to mask the smell of rotting vegetation and plunged the spade back into the earth.

Then it happened. Billy introduced the band and Sunday came blasting out of the tiny speaker.

That was more than three and a half decades ago and although the world has transformed beyond all recognition, one thing remains unchanged – Billy still supports local talent with all the enthusiasm and gusto of a fourth division football manager whose team had made it to the FA Cup Final.

Even though 'playlists' have been introduced and DJs instructed not to play songs outside the official Top 50, Billy often sticks his head on the block and plays a worthy song regardless.

"How will it ever become a hit if no one gets to hear it?"

Thanks Bill, as an ambassador for local talent you're the best we've ever had.

PAULINE DANIELS
COMEDIENNE AND ACTRESS

What can I say about Billy that hasn't already been said? Not a lot.

He has long supported local bands and variety acts and when it comes to musical knowledge I know none better.

He has never been a bullshitter, if he didn't like you, you knew about it and he's the same today.

He pulls no punches but if he did like you, he did what he could to help. He will always fit you in for an interview, five minutes on Billy's show is worth half a theatre full.

His listeners trust his judgment. I have spent many a happy time at Pontins working for him on his mad weekends – they are second to none. Although he is a bit tight when it comes to paying.

I am also a member of the FRO secret society with Billy, other members include his wife Lesley, Tom and Lyn Staunton and my husband. I would love to tell you what the society is about – but then I'd have to kill you.

All I can say is that Billy is a great ambassador for Merseyside and I am glad to know him.

All my love, Mrs Duval x

IAN MCNABB
MUSICIAN

Billy has been there from the beginning, tirelessly championing Liverpool music, from the birth of Merseybeat to playing the latest demo from a new band from Kirkby formed last month.

He loves music and, by God, he loves Liverpool.

And Liverpool loves him.

This is the story of a great Liverpudlian and a true blue.

Essential reading for anyone who ever cared about Liverpool and it's salty heart.

LYN STAUNTON
BILLY'S AGENT

My husband Tom and I each have a different relationship with Billy.

Billy is only four weeks older than Tom and both are Aquarius, Billy in January, Tom in February and, coincidently, both worked in the Anglo Overseas company in Water Street, Liverpool, about the same time when they were 15 years old, although this was only discovered after many nights out over food and drink.

They both love car boot sales and have spent many summer and winter mornings bringing home complete rubbish. Billy would turn up at 6am at our house and Tom would have a bacon butty ready for him before they went car booting. We have always said that if Billy Butler had not been in radio he would have been a multi-millionaire now as an antique dealer – the man knows what to buy and when to sell.

They love cowboy films and the TV series 24. Both drink bourbon and enjoy an occasional cigar and they both go to record fayres and have thousands of albums, CDs etc.

In fact, they really should have got married years ago as they only ever have an occasional row and you can bet it's Tom who gets annoyed at Billy, when BB wanders off at car boots or record fayres and gets immersed in what we call 'Billy's World.'

This is the place Billy goes to alone, his eyes glaze over and he forgets about the world around him.

To summarise they are two peas in a pod! To the annoyance of his wife Lesley and myself.

My relationship goes back many years with Billy as I was part of a sister act named 'The Mayer Sisters' who played cabaret clubs in the North West when Billy came into my life.

We were only very young. I was 16-years-old when my mother sent a demo record to Billy Butler on Radio Merseyside and – to her surprise – Billy played it many times and said how much he liked the record . . . that was like Simon Cowell today giving you a record contract.

The Mayer Sisters became quite famous in Liverpool and subsequently went on to appear all over the world and at the London Palladium twice – not bad for three little girls from Liverpool, and we always say that it was all down to Billy.

Billy was in all our homes everyday with that distinctive voice and we all thought we knew him – but I didn't really get to know him as a friend until many years later.

My associations with him came about through Power Promotions and my husband Tom and I representing the Billy & Wally Show that travelled clubs and theatres.

From this I was invited to appear on his radio show every Friday for many years, on a programme called: 'Stars in Their Ears', on which myself and local musician Bobby Sox would judge local music sent in by musicians and singer/songwriters.

I truly got to know the man and for that I am eternally grateful and privileged to know Billy Butler – the legend.

Bobby and I would get into the studio and be seated in front of Billy about 15 minutes before the show would go on air and sometimes Billy never said a word to either of us.

He never looked up – he would eat cherries and never offer any to me or Bobby. He would mess about with his head phones, then just as the red light came on to go live on air Billy would say: "Hiya" . . . this made Bobby and I laugh hysterically. Now, if you didn't know Billy, you could get offended by that, but we DO know him and he is so into what he is doing at that particular moment in time that he truly does not see or hear anything around him.

Power Promotions have represented Billy Butler for many years and never a contract was signed, for two reasons. One was trust and the other was you try getting Billy Butler's attention long enough.

Me, Tom, Billy and his wife Les have been friends for years and have shared many happy and sad times, and also played many practical jokes on each other.

We had a running gag for years involving a nude mannequin model acquired from a car boot sale.

That all started when Tom decided to put the said naked mannequin in Billy's front garden, legs facing up in the air in a 'V' sign, whilst he and Lesley were on holiday.

This has continued for years with the mannequin appearing in the most unexpected and embarrassing of places and sometimes fully dressed in Lesley's or my clothes. One day it actually had its own seat at a theatre show seated next to Billy.

Things went from bad to worse after that, but the very worse practical joke was on us.

Tom and I had planned to go to Arizona for a holiday and we had carefully booked great seats on the aircraft, booked a wonderful apartment in Scottsdale and our very good friends (the Butlers as we call them) very kindly offered to take us to the airport, although we declined the offer as we had booked a car to take us – well that's what friends are for, or so we thought.

We arrived at the airport and just as we were going through into the departures I was sure I'd seen two people who looked just like Billy and Lesley and to my utter amazement it WAS them.

To cut my long story very short, they had moved our seats on the aircraft and decided to jump in on our holiday – they had the cheek to try and take our bedroom in the apartment, but that failed and they spent the whole week on a sofa bed in the living room.

They slept in our room, ate our food, and videoed us when we both were ill in bed with food poisoning, and each night we could hear hysterical laughter in their room with them watching movies all night.

I am loathe to admit it but it was a brilliant holiday and I will take the sight of seeing Billy Butler in his boxie shorts first thing in the morning to the grave with me.

You cannot think of Liverpool without thinking of Billy Butler – he is Liverpool.

We have all grown up with him. We love him and hate him in equal measures. You can go all over the world and talk about the City of Liverpool and someone will mention Billy Butler.

BB never changes. He is opinionated and can infuriate you. He is gentle and sentimental and can endear you.

He can make you laugh and cry in the same five minutes just by touching your emotions through a song.

He can wish you happy birthday, or happy anniversary, and commiserate and console you when you need it most, but you will always feel special when he mentions your name, because he aims for your heart and he hits his target every time.

FRED LAWLESS
PLAYWRIGHT

Billy Butler has always been a man after my own heart – an Evertonian who loves music, comedy and his city.

I first met Billy in the early 1980s when I launched the UK's first kissogram company in Liverpool.

Billy loved the idea and featured our antics many times on his radio show, which was a great help in letting the public know about the weird and wonderful things we were getting up to.

Several years later, after having enjoyed many happy evenings chauffeuring beautiful girls around wearing sexy basques, stockings and suspenders (the girls also wore similar skimpy outfits!) I took up the pen and Billy was equally supportive, inviting me many times to come on his show to talk about new plays I'd written.

Billy's support was a great help in my early years as a playwright (and it still is!) and I know there are many people out there who are grateful for the 'leg up' Billy gave them by showcasing and supporting them. If John Peel was the champion of unknown bands then Billy Butler is the champion of unknown bands, writers, actors, singers, comedians etc etc.

Billy Butler has become a much loved institution on Merseyside. Whether he's playing music, interviewing guests, 'holding plums' or even helping Sophie from Speke sell a sofa, his radio shows are addictive and it will be a sad day if he ever decides to hang up his headphones.

Although those car boot sales probably won't know what's hit them!

BRIAN 'NASHER' NASH
MUSICIAN

Despite not living in Liverpool anymore, the first thing I do when I hit the M62 on a visit home is to tune into Billy.

A broadcasting legend and a champion of every Liverpool musician.

CHARLIE LANDSBOROUGH
MUSICIAN

In a world full of radio voices, Billy Butler is instantly recognisable, and his banter and humour have been putting smiles on faces of his listeners as long as I can remember.

He has always championed local causes and talent.

Billy has been a great supporter of artists and performers including myself.

He was playing my records when even I hadn't heard of myself.

Mrs Butler's Eldest once booked me to play at New Brighton's Floral Pavilion without telling me.

That's Billy.

Long may he continue.

BILL KENWRIGHT
FELLOW EVERTON FAN

Billy Butler is simply a life force.

He seems to have been around forever but still has the warmth, generosity of spirit, and enthusiasm he has always had.

On top of that, he is one of the very best radio presenters around – and the odd gift of a bit of 50s memorabilia from him pleases this fan enormously. Respect, Billy!

JANICE LONG
JOURNALIST

Billy was always on in the radio in our house. I was a teenager and Mum and Dad had a transistor which was always turned on for Billy's show, then turned off to save the batteries.

I never thought that I would get to meet and work with Billy, but I did, and thank the gods that our paths crossed.

What I love about Billy is his loyalty and generosity. We all know what an amazing broadcaster he is but not everyone knows what he is like when the mic is switched off.

When I joined BBC Radio Merseyside as a station assistant, working behind the scenes, Billy was the station's star. He was launching his career on national television too.

However he had time for rooky me and encouraged me in any way he could. He set me up with auditions for new TV programmes without me asking him and gave me tips on how to 'perform' on the radio.

I have always been grateful for his advice, support and generosity. I love his loyalty to Merseyside and its people.

We both love music and have a passion for finding new talent. Billy's ears are forever open and he is always there to give the bright young things a leg up.

So from me and everyone else you have helped along the way I would like to say thank you so much, Billy.

I know you are an MBE already as in Mrs Butler's Eldest, but just in case the Queen happens to be reading this on journeys to Balmoral and Badminton – any chance Billy Butler could be in your next honours list?

Billy Butler MBE . . . suits you!

SAM LEACH
AUTHOR AND FORMER PROMOTER

Billy and I go back a long way. He was the brightest wit on Juke Box Jury which was when I first saw his potential.

We met for the first time when he led his group The Tuxedos in a few shows for me at New Brighton Tower.

It didn't surprise me when he became a DJ and many times I've had to stop my car, laughing at his zany antics.

Billy discovered a good 'sidekick' in Wally and for years they kept Merseysiders splitting their sides with laughter.

Nowadays he keeps that standard flying high with the likes of 'Caring Steve' who just breaks me up.

And Billy has an encyclopedic knowledge of obscure artists and their work from years back. Mrs Butler's Eldest deserves all the recognition and praise he receives and the ultimate accolade of this book will prove that.

Billy – you've been a beacon on Liverpool's airwaves and will be for many years to come.

MIKE MCCARTNEY
PHOTOGRAPHER & AUTHOR

Mrs Butler's Eldest is like the Liver Birds and the Mersey Ferries.

He'll always be there.

Unlike the Overhead Railway and The Cavern.

He's never been demolished or filled in.

I've known him – like our kid – from the 60s, when he was in The Tuxedos.

BB is an institution.

People listen to him religiously – I choose my words carefully. The rock of Liverpool.

Right Billy, how about that tenner you promised me?

THREE LIVER BIRDS

SUZANNE COLLINS
ACTRESS

I grew up listening to Billy on the radio.

He's part of the family, so generous of spirit and as an actress it's fab that he not only previews shows but also comes and sees them, watches them and reviews them.

He is a person who personifies that great belief that values and principles still mean something.

EITHNE BROWNE
ACTRESS

He is someone who is a storyteller. He keeps the oral tradition alive.

Mrs Butler looking down on her son would be well proud.

Keep telling tales, Billy, and I don't mean snitching.

MARGI CLARKE
ACTRESS

Billy, you have made it possible for the people of Merseyside to share your microphone.

Everyone feels as if they have been on the Billy Butler show . . .

MICK ORD
STATION MANAGER, BBC RADIO MERSEYSIDE

Flashback to 1971. Hot Love by T Rex is Number One in the charts and Everton have just lost 1-0 at home to West Ham. What could be worse for a teenage would-be 'trog'? (my school would not allow us to have long hair.)

My mum had just returned from BBC Radio Merseyside's old studios in Sir Thomas Street in the city centre after a visit with her friends from the Union of Catholic Mothers.

Face aglow . . . "Guess who I've just met?"

"Marc Bolan? Alan Ball? Bill Shankly? Neil Armstrong, Frank Zappa?" said the permanently unimpressed, sulky 14-year-old.

"Billy Butler!!!" she splutteringly replied, with disgust at my insolence. "I got his autograph as well."

Flash-forward 40 years and I bet similar conversations are happening in households all over Merseyside, 2010-style. But back to '71.

Me: "What's he like?"

Mum: "Funny. And scruffy, with long hair."

Not much has changed. Well that's not fair, he's a really sharp dresser now – although the hair is no longer long – and I'm the scruff bag. Sorry mum (well done, Les.)

Mention local radio (never mind BBC Radio Merseyside) to people in this area and Billy Butler is always one of the first names to come to the lips. Usually followed by "I love him" or "I hate him."

The best broadcasters often polarise listeners (Ross, Evans, Blackburn, Moyles) and BB is no exception.

I wish I had a penny for everyone I've met who falls into the both categories, but the thing to remember is that the people who don't like him, still listen. When Chris Evans came into Radio Merseyside a few months ago to talk about his new book he treated Billy like an idol.

Quite right too. He is a nationally know local radio presenter and we are hugely proud of him.

Billy still makes thousands of Merseysiders laugh, cry or get angry between 2-5pm Monday to Friday every week of the year. He's lost none of his fire and his enthusiasm – if anything he is even more passionate about serving our audience than ever – and that should give us all hope!

He's a man who doesn't know what it's like NOT to feel passionate – about his family, his children's annual collection, his music, his football, his Merseyside . . .

But his passion is tempered by a lifetime's experience and knowledge that, deep down, it's PEOPLE that matter, not institutions, and he'll fight tooth and nail for ordinary people to have their voices heard – which in this day and age of iPods, and iPhones, Google and HDTV is comforting and invigorating at the same time.

This book is a deserved accolade for Mrs Butler's Eldest and long overdue.

Enjoy it and savour one of Merseyside's brightest gems. Long may he shine.

ARTHUR JOHNSON
JOURNALIST & PR GURU

I caused quite a storm when I was features editor of the Echo and signed Billy up for a weekly column.

I felt very strongly that the paper needed a 'Scouse voice' and that Billy, who was on Radio City at the time, would fit the bill perfectly.

However the traditional 'old hands' on the paper were horrified at the idea and made a point of letting me know!

As it turned out the column was incredibly popular attracting more letters than any other in the paper.

Each week I'd meet up with Billy in Vincent's Wine Bar in Old Hall Street to hand over dozens of letters from readers and discuss the content of his next column.

This routine continued when he moved to Radio Merseyside and I well remember him walking into Vincent's one day very excited. He'd just had the idea for a new quiz which he'd call Hold Your Plumbs.

The BBC will never allow that, I told him. He said it had been agreed that they'd try it out with the Radio Times listings and see what happened. The rest is history.

Billy has always been very supportive of all the charity appeals the paper has been involved in over the years.

He continues to support charities I am involved with.

MICHAEL STARKE
ACTOR

I don't know Billy well but I've been on his shows so many times, from the days with Andrew Schofield to my days on Brookside and Corrie.

I have been all over the country touring with musicals and you can come home and talk to him and he is knowledgeable about composers and writers from all genres.

He's never changed.

It's like seeing and talking to an old friend.

My dad, Sammy, would laugh his head off listening to Billy.

I think that's Billy's secret (if there is one) he's like someone you've known for years, then realise you don't.

When you are a young actor starting out and you need support you know he's got time for you.

On the radio he puts you at ease.

It's in his nature to plug and promote people and he's never faltered from that line of thinking.

He sums up what local radio is all about and yet he's a national broadcaster to us.

STAN BOARDMAN
ENTERTAINER

Billy Butler is a motor-mouth.

That brilliant man has household-name stars from all over the showbiz world on his programmes and he does one thing better than anybody else . . . he is the ultimate radio presenter who puts everyone on the same level.

He asks questions and then he answers them.

He'll have Tony Bennett on, Judy Collins or Neil Sedaka – you name them and they are there.

From actors to authors, comedians, musicians, sports people to poets and politicians.

But there's a clause – he asks the questions then answers the same questions.

Brilliant.

A great listener – unless you ask him to get a round in.

He's a Liverpool icon.

My mam used to want to know what frequency he was on because he kept moving from each local radio station.

I used to get the papers and mark out on the paper where he was in the schedules – my ma used to loved to hear him that much.

But he's a one-man radio show, BB – you don't need guests with Mrs Butler's Eldest.

PETE PRICE
BILLY'S GAY FRIEND/BROADCASTER/COLUMNIST/ STAND-UP COMIC AND PANTO QUEEN

I used to love listening to Billy Butler on the radio.

I still do unless I'm on air myself. Billy is a great 'wind up' merchant.

We were on New Brighton's Floral Pavilion doing panto and I was half dressed up – I was nearly made up. I sat there in my dressing room ready to play an ugly character (difficult for me).

But I had a lot of make-up on and Billy comes in, knocks on my door and says: "Pete, yer on."

Well I ran on stage and I wasn't due on for at least five minutes. Humiliation.

That's him.

He has done things like that all his life. A practical joker. A lover of libraries and car boot sales.

He knows music. I don't.

He does. End of story.

And he's a great broadcaster. A brave one not afraid to talk about anything.

I listened to him then and, like I said, I still do. That's the test of time.

I'm so glad he's touched my life.

MICKY FINN
COMEDIAN

Billy has played more clubs than I have.

What never ceases to amaze me about him is that he could bring anyone to Liverpool he wanted because they respect him.

I'm sure he manages The Drifters on the side, all 60 different versions.

Everyone knows who Billy is.

He has had acts on The Montrose and in his Pontin's shows who come because he's Billy Butler – now that's a great thing.

He has been so supportive to every up and coming comic and me. But you have a show on and he will plus it – he likes the underdog.

He helps people coming through the business.

Let's face it, he's been there, done that . . . seen it heard it and yet every time he does a show it's a brand new day for him.

Cracking feller.

GERRY MARSDEN
MUSICIAN

I am amazed that Billy Butler's show is fresh every day.

No two shows are the same.

We go back a long way to Cavern days and I knew then what a great personality he was.

He does a lot of things for charity – by that I mean he gives his time. He's a one off.

I want to know something Billy, give us a clue: "How do you do it? day in and day out?"

I don't know how but . . . I Like It . . .

Great, I've plugged two of my own songs.

Ta Billy.

OUTRO

Well that was it – that's the book – my gratitude goes
out to all my faithful listeners, without their input it
would not have been possible. To enjoy even more,
tune in to me each weekday on BBC Radio Merseyside
on 95.8 FM, 1485 AM, digital and online.
Have a look at my facebook page the
billybutlershow@facebook.com.
Hold your plums and Bradshaws DVDs are available at
the Radio Merseyside shop in Hanover Street.
(Part of the price of this book goes towards buying
Billy Bradshaw a budgie!)
The future . . . at my age – is there one?
But Never Doubt – Never Fear, as long as the BBC
want me I'll be there!

Billy Butler

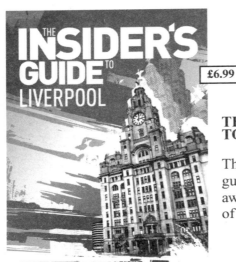

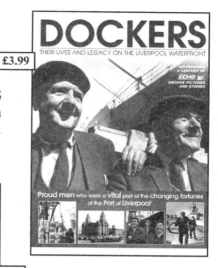

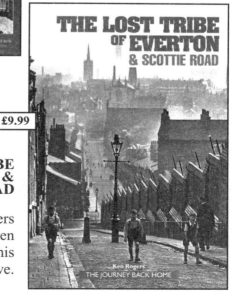

Can I leave you with the first three verses of a
beautiful poem 'The Dash' by Linda Ellis:

I read of a reverend who stood to speak at the
funeral of his friend. He referred to the dates on her
tombstone from the beginning . . . to the end.
He noted that first came the date of her birth and
spoke of the following date with tears, but he said
what mattered most of all was the dash between
those years. For that dash represents all the time
that she spent alive on earth . . . and now only those
who loved her know what that little line is worth.

I hope you've enjoyed part of my dash.
Billy Butler, MBE

Contents

Introduction	3
Bluebell beginnings	4
Sheffield Park station	6
Railway heritage	8
Historic locomotives	10
Sheffield Park to Horsted Keynes	14
Keeping things moving	18
Dinner is served	20
Horsted Keynes station	22
Illustrated route map	24
Celebrations	26
Carriage craftsmanship	28
Extending north: 1980-1994	32
Horsted Keynes to Kingscote	34
Wagons and freight	38
Kingscote station	42
Extending north: 1994-2013	44
Arriving at East Grinstead	46
Index of locomotives	48

© Keith Leppard 2013
First published in 2013
Reprinted 2014
Reprinted 2015

British Library Cataloguing in Publication Data
A catalogue record for this book is available from the
British Library.

Acknowledgments

I would like to thank the many photographers who
have generously allowed me to use their work in
this book. Without their presence to witness events
at the railway, both momentous and day-to-day, this
volume would have been immeasurably the poorer.
I should also apologise to all those who no doubt
have photographs much better than those of mine
that I have included, for not issuing a general call for
contributions; I plead lack of time and also an innate
dislike of making difficult decisions, which would
have been even more necessary with a wider field of
images from which to choose. I also want to thank
Roger Price, Colin Tyson and Russell Pearce for their
time spent proof-reading the manuscript, and Nikki
Favell for her support with the project. Above all, I
want to thank the many people who give so freely of
their spare time to volunteer at the railway. Without
them, the story that is told in this book would have
ended many years ago.

Keith Leppard

ISBN 978 1 85794 391 7

Silver Link Publishing Ltd
The Trundle
Ringstead Road
Great Addington
Kettering
Northants NN14 4BW

Tel/Fax: 01536 330588
email: sales@nostalgiacollection.com
Website: www.nostalgiacollection.com

Printed and bound in Česká Republika

About the author

Keith Leppard has been a life-long steam enthusiast
with a particular passion for the Bluebell Railway. It
was his local preserved railway during his childhood
and he began volunteering there in the fledgling
Carriage & Wagon Department in 1970. Even
though work later took him away from the area
and from active volunteering, he has remained a
very engaged 'armchair' member of the Bluebell
Railway Preservation Society ever since. His early
involvement with carriage restoration sparked a
particular admiration for the craftsmanship and
engineering in carriages of the steam era. This is his
first railway book.

Front cover: **THE BLUEBELL IN SPRING** On a
beautiful spring day in May 2012, Southern Railway
Class 'U' No 1638 makes a fine sight as it takes its
northbound six-coach train, all in 1930s SR lined
olive-green livery, past a bank of spring flowers near
Birchstone Bridge, between Horsted Keynes and
Kingscote. *Paul Pettitt*

Frontispiece: **THE BLUEBELL IN AUTUMN**
LBSCR Class 'A1' No 672 *Fenchurch* catches the low
autumn sun in November 2006 as it heads a train
of Victorian carriages south past Tremains, between
Horsted Keynes and Sheffield Park. This was a 'top
and tail' service; sister engine No 55 *Stepney* is
assisting on the rear of the train. *Jon Bowers*

Introduction

In 1959 a small band of enthusiasts, foreseeing the end of steam power on Britain's railways, came together 'to preserve the puffer for posterity'. Their focus was a recently closed route that ran northwards from the Sussex coast at Lewes through the Ouse valley and then the Sussex Weald to the town of East Grinstead. Having first hoped to reopen the entire line, practicalities forced them to settle for operating a 5-mile stretch from Sheffield Park to Horsted Keynes. The Bluebell Railway began public services over this route on 7 August 1960, becoming the first standard-gauge preserved passenger line in the country. From those beginnings, a major part of the Bluebell story from the mid-1970s onwards has been its efforts to reopen the route north from this original section. These efforts culminated recently in the return of steam trains to East Grinstead, with public operations beginning in 2013.

The future Bluebell Railway route began life with the incorporation of the Lewes & East Grinstead Railway by Act of Parliament in 1877. This company amalgamated with the main railway operator in the area, the London, Brighton & South Coast Railway (LBSCR), in 1878, which then built the line. It opened to the public on 1 August 1882, serving stations at Barcombe, Newick & Chailey, Sheffield Park, Horsted Keynes, West Hoathly and Kingscote. A branch from Horsted Keynes westwards to the LBSCR main line at Haywards Heath was opened in September 1883 with one intermediate station at Ardingly.

The line was provided with lavish, ornate stations and the earthworks, bridges and tunnels were built for double track, though only East Grinstead to Haywards Heath was ever laid as such. Sheffield Park and Newick & Chailey had passing loops, and all the stations had sidings and facilities for handling goods. The promoters of the line hoped there would be substantial freight traffic, and milk was indeed a major source of revenue for many years. The prospects still looked bright when the branch from Haywards Heath to Horsted Keynes was electrified in 1935; there were post-war plans to extend this northwards to East Grinstead, but these never materialised.

In fact, traffic on the future Bluebell line had already dwindled in the face of competition from road haulage, and official recognition of this came with its first closure in 1955. However, Miss Bessemer, a local resident, protested that the 1877 Act required a certain number of passenger trains to be run, so some services had to be reinstated while the Act was repealed; final closure took place on 16 March 1958. Miss Bessemer's intervention may only have provided a temporary reprieve, but it proved invaluable in the formation of the Bluebell Railway. Without her it is unlikely that the closure of a sleepy Sussex branch line would have come to wide public attention and the enthusiast flame might never have been lit. More than 50 years later, the Bluebell Railway is a large and thriving enterprise that has just achieved its ambition to reconnect with the main railway network.

Being so early in the field of railway preservation, the Bluebell was able to acquire many historic steam locomotives, carriages and wagons, often directly from service with British Railways. With other owner societies coming subsequently to join the Bluebell community with their prized possessions, the railway is now home to a magnificent collection that dates back to the 1860s, mostly from the railway companies that operated in southern England. The Bluebell aims to run regular service trains that reflect the different eras represented in this collection, so visitors frequently have the chance to experience trains that are more than 100 years old.

This book brings you this Bluebell journey – both along the line and through its first 50 years – in pictures. Enjoy the ride!

LBSCR No 672 *Fenchurch* passes Ketches Halt with a 'Bluebells' special in 2006. *Dave Phillips*

Bluebell Beginnings

Right: **THE VERY BEGINNING!** After the initial meetings and discussions, the first Bluebell rolling stock arrived at the railway on 17 May 1960. Southern Railway Brake Composite No 6575, built in 1929, and London & South Western Railway non-corridor Lavatory 3rd No 320, built in 1900, were headed by LBSCR 'A1X' No 55, formerly named *Stepney*. They came over the still operational Ardingly branch and are seen here heading south out of Horsted Keynes onto Bluebell metals for the first time. *Bluebell Railway Archive (J. L. Smith)*

Below: **PREPARING FOR THE PUBLIC** A lot needed to be done to get ready for the first Bluebell Railway passenger service, which ran on 7 August 1960. Much as happens when a business changes ownership today, corporate branding was not neglected. The engines were left in black livery, but were re-lined and prominently named on the tanks, while the coaches were transformed into Bluebell blue livery. Here, the railway's second locomotive, South Eastern & Chatham Railway (SECR) Class 'P' No 323 *Bluebell* poses with coach 320 in July 1960 while work continues on the second vehicle, 6575. *Ron Fisher*

Below right: **BLUEBELL HALT** During the 1960/61 seasons, public trains were only allowed as far north as Bluebell Halt, a temporary wooden platform located a short distance south of the junction at Horsted Keynes. Trains only began running into Horsted Keynes station – still shared with the British Railways service on the Ardingly branch – on 29 October 1961, the last day of the season. *Bluebell Archive*

Right: **EARLY ARRIVALS** SECR 'P' Class No 27 arrived at the railway in the spring of 1961 and was immediately christened *Primrose* to match its sister engine No 323 *Bluebell*. However, for the 1963 season No 27 was repainted into lined SECR passenger livery, losing its name in the process, and ran in this guise until the mid-1970s. It is seen here with the railway's two SECR carriages on a southbound service of that period. Repairs to No 27 were started in the 1980s but proved too complex, so the engine was set aside as a kit of parts, work only recommencing in 2012. *Bluebell Archive (David Christie)*

Below left: **EARLY ARRIVALS** The LBSCR ancestry of the Bluebell line meant that in its early days the railway was keen to obtain LBSCR locomotives. But after No 55 *Stepney* it had to wait until October 1962 for the arrival of LBSCR Class 'E4' No 473 *Birch Grove* – the sixth locomotive acquired. Built in 1898, No 473 was soon repainted into the umber livery of the LBSCR in the early 20th century and is seen here waiting to leave Horsted Keynes in the mid-1960s. *Bluebell Archive (Ken Chown)*

Below right: **EARLY ARRIVALS** LSWR radial tank No 488 (BR No 30583, built in 1885) came to the railway in 1961, and the LBSCR Directors' Saloon No 60 arrived in 1964. Pictured here at Sheffield Park in August 1973, after No 488 had returned from overhaul at Swindon, both are considered to be among the gems of the railway's collection but have sadly been out of use for many years. *Bluebell Archive (S. C. Nash)*

Sheffield Park Station

Right: **SHEFFIELD PARK STATION** is painted in the colours of the LBSCR, the company that ran the line from its opening. As much as possible of the original station has been preserved, although, as the headquarters of the railway, there has been considerable development over the past 50 years to turn it from a wayside station into a busy railway terminus. Among these changes was the building of a large buffet and a shop, both of which are accessed from Platform 1, and a museum located on Platform 2 (see page 8). Sheffield Park is also home to the railway's locomotive works and shed (see page 10), the latter being open to visitors for viewing of locomotives that are not in service. *Keith Leppard*

Below: **EARLY START** The original enclosed timber footbridge at the north end of Sheffield Park station was demolished in the 1940s, leaving passengers to use a foot crossing. Forty years later, the Bluebell put up a replacement at the southern end of the station, which had previously been located at Lingfield station, on the route north from East Grinstead towards London. The footbridge now provides an excellent vantage point from which to view train movements at the station. In this early morning view, LBSCR 'Terrier' No 55, temporarily in BR livery as No 32655, simmers in Platform 2 on 14 January 2012 with a single-coach train formed of SECR 'Birdcage' Brake No 3363. These carriages get their nickname from the raised glazed section in the roof over the guard's accommodation. An elevated seat allows the guard a view in both directions to monitor the security of the train while in motion. *Dave Bowles*

Above: **SHEFFIELD PARK STATION** The Platform 2 canopy was rebuilt and extended for 2012. This picture of it from 19 May 2012 features one of the station's traditional gas lights. Recently restored SECR Brake 3rd No 3363 and LBSCR 'E4' No 473, both in SR lined olive-green livery, complete the scene. *Keith Leppard*

Far left: **SHEFFIELD PARK STATION** Seen from the public viewing area at the north end of Platform 2, Great Western Railway 'Dukedog' Class No 9017 *Earl of Berkeley*, here in the BR livery it carried from 2009 to 2011, waits to depart on 12 March 2011. *Keith Leppard*

Left: **SHEFFIELD PARK SIGNAL BOX** Unusually, the signal cabin at Sheffield Park is situated on the former down platform, which gives passengers the chance to watch the signalman at work while they wait for their train. The illuminated detector light in the station diagram above the instrument shelf shows that the Platform 1 track is currently occupied. *Keith Leppard*

Railway Heritage

A visit to the Bluebell Railway is so much more than a train ride. Great attention is paid to creating an experience of a bygone era, from the detail of the staff uniforms to the dressing of the stations with period advertisements and accessories.

Below: **A TICKET TO TREASURE** Traditional Edmondson tickets, which the Bluebell produces using an original printing machine, were introduced in the 1840s and used on Britain's railways through to 1990. Tickets are pre-printed on stiff card rectangles, each with a unique serial number, and are date-stamped by the booking clerk at the time of sale. This picture shows the date-stamping process and (inset) a ticket for an adult return trip from Sheffield Park to Kingscote in 3rd Class. *Keith Leppard*

Above: **RAILWAY MUSEUM** A new museum opened in 2012, housed in an extension to the former up platform waiting room at Sheffield Park. It was built as part of a project funded by the Heritage Lottery Fund to provide covered storage for the railway's operating carriages behind Platform 2. The museum's displays show smaller artefacts and interpret railway operations for visitors. *Keith Leppard*

Right: **RED FOR DANGER** A signal box, originally located at Withyham on the former east-west route from East Grinstead to Eridge, has been re-erected at the north end of the museum. It contains a small lever frame that visitors can try out under supervision while watching the trains depart. SR 'U' Class No 1638 is seen here leaving the station on 17 September 2012. *Keith Leppard*

MIXED TRAFFIC As well as preserving heritage locomotives and rolling stock, the railway also aims to conserve and demonstrate modes of railway operation from the past. Here SECR 'P' Class No 178 (built in 1910) hauls a mixed train typical of railway operations on branch lines in the Victorian & Edwardian eras; it includes LBSCR 1st No 661 (1880), LCDR Brake 3rd No 114 (1889) and assorted wagons. The train is approaching Horsted Keynes on 12 March 2011. *Keith Leppard*

Historic Locomotives

The Bluebell collection spans almost 90 years of development of the railway steam locomotive in the UK from the oldest – LBSCR 'Terrier' No 672 *Fenchurch*, an example of a design from the mid-Victorian era that was built in 1872 – through to a member of the last steam locomotive class to be built for Britain's railways – BR Class 9F No 92240, which left Crewe Works in 1958.

Below: **SHEFFIELD PARK YARD** This aerial view, taken on 29 March 2012, shows the yard backed by the running shed, locomotive works and, on the right, 'Atlantic House'. 'E4' No B473 is in the foreground and 'P' Class tanks Nos 178 and 323 to the right. To the left are No 3 *Captain Baxter* behind diesel shunter No 13236, and Class 4 tank No 80151. At the back are the boilerless engine of 'S15' No 847, in the works for major overhaul at the time, and the engine of 'Q' Class No 541 with the tender from 'U' Class No 1618. The large locomotive in the centre behind No B473 is 9F No 92212, visiting from the Mid-Hants Railway at the time. It is not practical or affordable to have all of the collection available for service at any given time, and many out-of-service locomotives are on display in the running shed. *Martin Lawrence*

Left: **No 4 SHARPTHORN** This diminutive locomotive has never steamed on the Bluebell Railway, yet holds a unique and crucial place in its history. Built in 1877, it was used by the original contractors during the construction of the line in 1882. A century later it was brought to the Bluebell and is pictured here at Horsted Keynes where it is normally on display. *Derek Hayward*

Below: **NORTH LONDON RAILWAY No 2650** Built at Bow Works in 1880, this locomotive arrived at the railway in working order in 1962. It also has a unique role in Bluebell history as it was loaned to contractors who were dismantling the line north from Horsted Keynes in 1964. After many years out of use, it was returned to service in its BR livery as No 58850 from 1984 to 1993, in time for it to play an important part in Bluebell's rebuilding of that same route. It is pictured here at Horsted Keynes. *Bluebell Archive*

Above: **NIGHT STEAM** A dark wet night only adds to the atmosphere of steam operations. BR Standard Class 5MT No 73082 *Camelot*, built in 1955, stands at Sheffield Park on 3 November 2004. *Dave Bowles*

Below: **CLASSIC GOODS** Maunsell's version of the classic 0-6-0 goods design for the Southern Railway was the 'Q' Class. Built in 1939, No 541 was in Bluebell service from 1983 to 1993, and is pictured at Sheffield Park in May 1990. *Tony Page*

Above: **LBSCR VETERANS** More recently seen on the line in BR lined black and SR lined olive-green liveries, perennial favourite 'E4' 0-6-2T No 473 *Birch Grove* is pictured here at Sheffield Park in 2002 paired with 'A1' No 672 *Fenchurch*, both in the LBSCR's umber livery of the early 1900s. *Keith Leppard*

Below: **SLEEPING GIANTS** In 2005/6, 30 years after the structure was first erected, the locomotive running shed was completed with a brick side wall that includes windows to a traditional design. Here two out-of-service locomotives, BR Standard Class 4MT No 75027 and Class 9F No 92240, stand outside the shed in October 2010. *Keith Leppard*

Keeping steam locomotives running requires a host of heavy engineering skills and facilities that were commonplace in Britain during the steam era but nowadays are a niche market at best. The Bluebell – in common with other preserved lines – has to scour the country and beyond for commercial fabrication of parts as well as doing a multitude of engineering tasks in-house. The locomotive works at Sheffield Park was built in 1975 and has since been extended twice – but it is still too small to cope easily with the work required, much of which is still done outside in the yard.

Below: **BOILER REPAIRS** Locomotives require a heavy overhaul after every 10 years of service. The boiler is removed from the frames, inspected and repaired to satisfy the boiler inspector. At the same time other necessary repairs will be done to the engine (cylinders, motion, frames, etc) to give hopefully 10 more years of reasonably trouble-free use. Here the boiler from SECR 'H' Class No 263 is under repair during 2011, with the boiler of SR 'S15' Class No 847 in the background. *Dave Phillips*

Right: **RESTORATION PROJECT** Standard Class 4 tank No 80100 is one of only three steam locomotives at the railway never to have operated there. Seen here in the running shed in August 2010, during the railway's 50th anniversary celebrations, it is still in the condition in which it arrived in 1978 from a scrapyard in South Wales, where it had spent more than a decade. It makes quite a contrast with its sister locomotives No 80064 (posed behind it) and No 80151 (see page 21); restoring a locomotive from this condition to working order is a major task! *Derek Hayward*

Right: **BUILDING FROM NEW** Undoubtedly the biggest locomotive engineering project on the Bluebell Railway to date is the construction of a new Class 'H2' LBSCR 'Atlantic' (the railway term for a 4-4-2 wheel arrangement). The project was launched in 1987 with the intention of using an existing boiler from a related Great Northern Railway locomotive. As shown here, by the summer of 2012 a brand new set of frames and cylinders had been produced, but it will be several years yet before No 32424 *Beachy Head* is finished. *Fred Bailey*

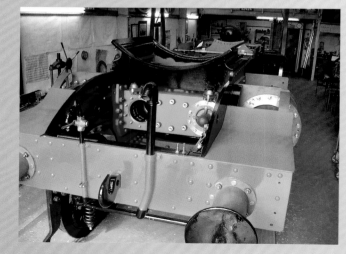

SR CLASS USA No 30064 This locomotive is of a North American design and was bought by the Southern Railway at the end of the Second World War. It came to the Bluebell in 1971 and entered service immediately, working until 1984 with only a brief pause for overhaul. Seen here in a BR-style green livery, it is now displayed in War Department grey as No WD1959, awaiting its turn for repair. *Bluebell Archive*

Above right: **SECR CLASS 'H' No 263** The powerful Class 'H' tank engines were built in the 1900s for heavy suburban traffic in SE London and later migrated to country branch lines as electrification progressed. No 263 ended up very close to the Bluebell, working between East Grinstead and Three Bridges until 1964, when it was withdrawn. Coming to the Bluebell in 1975, it is pictured here on 28 July 2012, immaculately turned out in fully lined SECR passenger livery as it began its third period of service on the railway. *Martin Lawrence*

Right: **SR CLASS 'V' 'SCHOOLS' No 928 *STOWE*** The 'Schools' Class was designed originally to operate the route from London to Hastings via Tonbridge, which had an exceptionally narrow loading gauge because of short-cuts taken during its construction. Introduced in 1930, the 'Schools' were the most powerful 4-4-0 locomotives ever built and proved so successful that in the end they were used widely across the Southern network. No 928 *Stowe* arrived at the Bluebell in 1980 and operated for much of that decade, being seen here on the approach to Horsted Keynes. *Bluebell Archive (David Christie)*

POLEAY BRIDGE Leaving Sheffield Park the railway crosses the River Ouse, then Poleay Bridge, where views of trains taken from the west, particularly in the late afternoon, are a favourite with the railway's many lineside photographers. Here SECR 'C' Class No 592, reflected in the flood from the river, departs with a train formed of BR Mark 1 stock on 17 January 2010. *Jon Bowers*

Left: **FRESHFIELD BANK** The journey to Horsted Keynes, which takes about 15 minutes, is uphill most of the way. Following the River Ouse upstream from Sheffield Park, crews quickly have to tackle Freshfield Bank, which, at a gradient of 1 in 75, is steep in railway terms. SR 'U' Class No 1638 gets to grips with the ascent on a heavy Santa Special working in December 2009. *Ian Wright*

Below left: **FRESHFIELD BANK** BR Class 5MT No 73082 *Camelot,* which was named in 1959 following the withdrawal of the 'King Arthur' Class locomotive of that name, is starting the climb in an undated picture taken between 1995 and 2000. During the 1990s the railway operated a set of BR Mark 1 coaches in maroon livery. This livery was used throughout much of the UK from the mid-1950s, with locomotives in lined black or Brunswick green, until British Railways switched to blue and grey livery for its carriages at the end of steam in the late 1960s. *Bluebell Archive*

Above: **TREMAINS** In April 2011, wending their way through woodlands near Tremains, midway between Sheffield Park and Horsted Keynes, lucky passengers on a southbound 'Bluebell Special' get to see just how the railway got its name. The train is hauled, appropriately, by SECR Class 'P' No 323 *Bluebell. Andrew Strongitharm*

Left: **TOWN PLACE** The line levels out between Town Place bridge and Tremains. Former LSWR Adams radial tank No 488, built in 1885 and running here in BR livery as No 30583, is approaching Freshfield Lane in the gentle light of late autumn 1983. *Bluebell Archive (Peter Zabek)*

Above right: **KEYSFORD LANE BRIDGE** No 488 has just passed Keysford Lane with a northbound train in 1988. The short-lived Holywell Halt was located here for the 1962 season. No 488 owes its survival to the demands of working the Lyme Regis branch, for which it and two sister engines were kept in service until the 1960s. Its LSWR pea-green livery is contemporary with the salmon and bitter chocolate used on coach No 1520 (see page 30). *Bluebell Archive (Peter Constable)*

Left: **CASEFORD BRIDGE** Another 1 in 75 climb takes the line north towards Caseford Bridge and Horsted Keynes. The railway's former GWR 'Dukedog' Class locomotive, No 9017 *Earl of Berkeley*, pictured here in GWR livery, passes with a northbound train in February 2005. *Paul Pettitt*

Below: **THREE ARCH BRIDGE** On the approach to Horsted Keynes the view of trains on the embankment between Three Arch Bridge and New Road Bridge in the afternoon light is another classic Bluebell scene. Here SECR Class 'O1' 0-6-0 No 65, rebuilt in 1908 from an 1896 SER Class 'O' design, heads north on 9 March 2009. At this time No 65 was nearing the end of a 10-year period of very reliable service on the railway. Harry Wainwright's SECR designs shared several distinctive features, and the 'O1' rebuild appears very similar to his own 'C' Class 0-6-0 design (see page 40), the most visible difference being the smaller tender of the 'O1', with external springs. *Jon Bowers*

Above: **THREE ARCH BRIDGE** The distinctive form of Three Arch Bridge marks the start of the approach to Horsted Keynes. Northbound trains are still working hard as they pass the bridge, but here former LBSCR 'E4' No B473 is running with the grade on a southbound train formed mostly of SR Maunsell-era carriages. *Len Walton*

Left: **SUSSEX FLASHBACK** SR Class 'U' No 1618 crosses Keysford Lane Bridge with a northbound service while a vintage bus passes below. This springtime scene was captured in 1983. *Bluebell Archive*

Keeping thing moving

As well as the historic locomotives, carriages and stations, a visit to the Bluebell is about the people who make it all happen. The staff, from those in the public eye such as locomotive crew, guards, station staff, signalmen and in the shops and buffet to those toiling behind the scenes on track, locomotive, carriage and signal maintenance, are mostly volunteers.

Right: **FOOTPLATE DUTIES** During 2007 rebuilt SR 'West Country' Class Bulleid 'Pacific' No 34028 *Eddystone* was operating at the railway on extended loan. These images show a view of the footplate on 15 July, and the crew at Horsted Keynes on 12 August with single-line token in hand. *Jon Bowers/Keith Leppard*

Below: **HEAVY WORK** Building and maintaining the infrastructure of the line can be heavy work, and often has to take place in locations remote from the road. The railway owns a 45-ton Ransomes & Rapier steam breakdown crane, built in 1942, which was based during its working life at Gorton and Newton

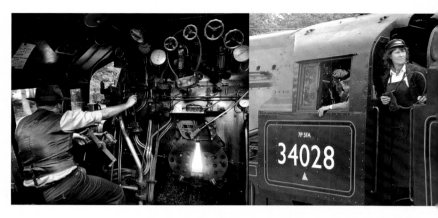

Heath depots in Manchester. It has been used on a variety of tasks since arriving at the Bluebell in 1981 and is seen here removing a large redundant signal post from the lineside on Freshfield Bank in April 1987. *Tony Sullivan*

Right: **TRAFFIC AND SIGNALS** In July 2007 the guard on a southbound service at Horsted Keynes gives the 'right away' to the loco crew, while in September 2012 (*centre right*) the platform staff at Sheffield Park indicate that a northbound train is ready to depart. Access for trains onto each single-line section is controlled by a token, and in the third picture (*far right*) the crew of a northbound service exchange the southern section token for the northern one with the Horsted Keynes signalman on 22 January 2012. *Jon Bowers/ Keith Leppard/Martin Lawrence*

Right and far right: **MAINTAINING THE TRACK** This is a never-ending task, carried out in all weathers. On a snowy 6 April 2008 three hardy souls do some routine maintenance at Ingwersen's curve, while amid the distractions of a beautiful spring day on 28 May 2006 the track on Freshfield bank receives attention. *Both Jon Bowers*

Dinner is served

Below: **PULLMAN STYLE** From the end of the 19th century, long-distance trains started to convey restaurant cars that offered meals served by waiters with all the style of the most reputable city eating establishments. This service reached its pinnacle in the opulent surroundings of the Pullman cars, amply illustrated by the interior of the Bluebell's 1st Class Parlour Kitchen Car *Fingall*, built in 1924, with tables laid for full service. *Richard Salmon*

Above: **PULLMAN DINING**
Guests are well into their lunch as the southbound 'Golden Arrow' passes Horsted Keynes on 12 August 2007.

Right: As this picture of the interior of *Christine* shows, even Pullman 3rd Class is quite sumptuous! *Both Keith Leppard*

Below: **SERVICE WITH A SMILE**
Pullman service doesn't just include good food in extravagant surroundings. Welcome aboard! *Derek Hayward*

PULLMAN STYLE While 1st Class Pullman Cars were always known by name, their 3rd Class counterparts had numbers only. However, the two 3rd Class Pullmans in service at the Bluebell, formerly Cars No 64 and 76, have been named *Christine* and *Lilian* respectively.

GOLDEN ARROW The Southern Railway's all-Pullman 'Golden Arrow' service, which operated from London to Dover for onward service to the continent, gained worldwide fame. This train is commemorated by the Bluebell Railway's own 'Golden Arrow' dining service.

Right: The up 'Arrow' passes the Kingscote Distant signal in April 2008, hauled by 'West Country' Class 4-6-2 No 21C123 *Blackmore Vale*. The distinctive air-smoothed casing of this type of locomotive, which was often used by the SR on the 'Golden Arrow', allows the train's insignia to be displayed to full effect. *Paul Pettitt*

Below: The up 'Arrow' again, this time approaching Horsted Keynes on 25 July 2010 hauled by rebuilt 'Battle of Britain' Class 4-6-2 No 34059 *Sir Archibald Sinclair*. *Martin Lawrence*

Below right: A down 'Golden Arrow' working approaches Horsted Keynes in the charge of BR Standard Class 4 tank No 80151 on 12 August 2007. *Keith Leppard*

Horsted Keynes station

HORSTED KEYNES is a large country station with five platforms, dock and goods yards. The railway's Carriage & Wagon Department is based here and a viewing gallery in the works is normally open to visitors.

Below: The station area viewed from the north in 2010. The line to Sheffield Park is in the centre while the route of the former branch to Haywards Heath passes behind the signal box. When Bluebell services began, this branch was still being operated by British Railways electric trains.

The Bluebell owns the trackbed as far as Ardingly and it is hoped that one day its operations will extend over that route too. *Keith Leppard*

Right: **HORSTED KEYNES** The decorative tiling on the walls of the main station building is typical of traditional buildings in this part of Sussex, while the gardens on the platforms add to the station's charm. The railway's immaculately restored SR Maunsell coaches complete the springtime scene. *Len Walton*

Below: Pictured in the evening sunshine on 21 August 2005, southbound trains headed by BR Class 4 tank No 80151 and 'E4' Class No 32473 in BR livery stand at Platforms 3 and 4/5 respectively. The buildings and canopy on Platforms 1 and 2 were demolished by the LBSCR in 1914, and carefully reinstated between 1992 and 2005 to match the originals. *Jon Bowers*

Below: **SIGNAL BOX**
The southern end of Horsted Keynes station is commanded by an impressive signal box, and every one of its 40 levers is needed to control the complex track and signalling at the station. Here LBSCR 'Terrier' No 672 *Fenchurch*, in the livery it carried at the railway for most of the years up until 2001, is getting some admiration as it sits in Platform 1 with the GNR Directors' Saloon during the 1980s. *Bluebell Archive (David Christie)*

Above left: **PLATFORMS 3 AND 4** provide the focus for most of the passenger activity at Horsted Keynes on normal operating days. When trains on the single line cross there, the station becomes a temporary hive of activity. Between trains, passengers can linger at the bookstall or buffet, both of which are preservation items in their own right. On 23 May 2010 No 672 *Fenchurch* is providing the added distraction of brake van rides along the Ardingly spur. *Martin Lawrence*

Above right: **PERIOD DETAIL** Horsted Keynes station is preserved in the early Southern Railway period, c1930. Many artefacts help to re-create that bygone era. *Keith Leppard*

Right: Entering the booking hall on a winter's day is like stepping back in time, with an open coal fire to warm travellers while they buy their tickets. And in the adjacent waiting room there is a telephone where users had to press buttons A and B long before mobile phones were dreamed of! *Keith Leppard*

EAST GRINSTEAD

2013

Mainline Rail

Hill Place (Imberhorne) Viaduct

Hill Place Farm

Imberhorne Lane Bridge

Hazelden Farm Bridge

Vowels Lane Bridge

Turners Hill Road Bridge

Kingscote 1994

Mill Place Bridge

Birch Farm Crossing

Birchstone Bridge

Ingwersen's

New Coombe Bridge

Site of West Hoathly Station

1992

West Hoathly

Sharpthorne

Tunnel

Vaux End Bridge

Black Hut

Dates along the route indicate the first opening of the Bluebell to that point from the south (Sheffield Park).

Leamland Bridge

Horsted House Farm Bridge

Horsted Keynes

New Road Bridge

Three Arch Bridge (Nobles')

Keysford Lane Bridge (Holywell Waterworks')

Caseford Bridge

Tremaines

Lindfield Wood

Monteswood Lane Bridge

Freshfield Lane Bridge

Town Place Bridge

Oakham Bridge

Ketches Wood

Freshfield Bank

River Ouse flood plain

Poley Bridge

Ouse Bridge

A275

Sheffield Park

1960

1961

1960

Images from Dave Bowles, Mike Esau, Derek Hayward, Keith Leppard, Paul Pettitt and Ian Wright.

Celebrations

Right: **GIANTS OF STEAM 2007** With the Bluebell's own No 21C123 *Blackmore Vale* in service and No 34028 *Eddystone* at the railway for the year, October 2007 was the ideal chance to create a line-up of O. V. S. Bulleid's 'West Country'/'Battle of Britain' Class 4-6-2 locomotives. No 34007 *Wadebridge* (left) and No 34081 *92 Squadron* (right), visiting for the occasion, stand with Nos 34028 and 21C123 at the north end of Horsted Keynes station against the setting sun on 19 October. *Derek Hayward*

Right: '**TERRIER**' **GALA 2006** Built in the 1870s, the LBSCR 'Terriers' are great survivors. As well as the Bluebell's No 55 *Stepney* and No 672 *Fenchurch*, eight others still exist, and in November 2006 three visitors joined the residents in a 'Terrier' gala. From the left, Nos 32678 (formerly *Knowle*), W8 *Freshwater* (formerly 646 *Newington*) and 662 *Martello* pose with *Stepney* and *Fenchurch* at the north end of Horsted Keynes station. *Jon Bowers*

50th ANNIVERSARY OF THE BLUEBELL 6-8 August 2010

Right: A re-creation of the railway's first public train departs from Sheffield Park. No 55 *Stepney* is in its 1960 livery, while coaches Nos 1098 and 6686 substitute for the original 320 and 6575. At the rear of the train No 672 *Fenchurch* stands in for No 323 *Bluebell*, which was not in service at the time. *Derek Hayward*

Below right: The traditional celebratory cavalcade of all available locomotives at Horsted Keynes. From left to right, they are LBSCR No 55 *Stepney* and No 672 *Fenchurch*, SECR Nos 178 and 592, 'E4' No B473, Class 'U' No 1638 and No 34059 *Sir Archibald Sinclair*. When this many locomotives all whistle together they can really make themselves heard! *Martin Lawrence*

Carriage craftsmanship

The Bluebell's collection contains some 80 carriages that span a century of design development. Only the earliest arrivals, together with some of the newer BR Mark I coaches that came later, were in a condition fit to run and these all required major work within a decade or so. Others were derelict, often lacking their interior fittings and, for most of the Victorian coaches, their underframes and running gear too. So far only a little more than half have been used in passenger service, mostly following extensive rebuilding and restoration.

Right: **SECR No 3360** Railway coachbuilding continued the tradition of craftsmanship found in the horse-drawn carriages that were being superseded, and these traditions are maintained by the Bluebell's Carriage & Wagon Department today. During 2010/11 No 3360 was converted to provide a saloon for disabled visitors, with support from The Big Lottery Fund through its 'People's Millions' programme. It carries SECR crimson lake livery, contemporary with the ornate lined green seen on the railway's SECR locomotives. A coach will need at least 15 coats of paint, filler and varnish to produce a finish you can see your reflection in. *Keith Leppard*

Left: **CARRIAGE WORKS** Carriages comprise a body frame clad with external and internal panelling, mounted on an underframe. The wheels are either directly mounted on the underframe – the earliest design – or carried on two bogies that swivel at either end of the coach. This view of the Horsted Keynes carriage works, taken from the public viewing area in 2011, shows work completed on the framework of LBSCR four-wheel Brake 3rd No 949, originally constructed in 1881. *Keith Leppard*

METROPOLITAN RAILWAY COACHES In 1961 the railway acquired a set of four coaches built in 1898/1900 that had most recently been operating on the Chesham branch of London Underground's Metropolitan Line. Their arrival added much-needed passenger capacity and they bore the brunt of the traffic until around 1968, when their increasing dilapidation caused them to be laid aside. After many years of work the two outer coaches of the set – Brake 3rd No 387 and Full 3rd No 394 – were returned to traffic in 1999; Composite 1st/3rd No 368 followed in 2002, and Composite No 412 completed the set in 2006.

These coaches returned to the Metropolitan Line in central London in January 2013 as part of steam-hauled special trains to celebrate the 150th anniversary of the London Underground.

Above right: No 412 is seen at Kingscote on 12 August 2007 displaying an exquisite varnished teak finish. *Keith Leppard*

The interiors of all but the newest (50-year-old!) coaches tend to be visions of richly varnished woodwork, brightly polished brass or chrome fittings and padded seating trimmed in moquette to an authentic pattern.

Right and far right: Here we see 1st Class and 3rd Class compartments of No 412. In addition to a carpet, 1st Class passengers get wider and more deeply padded seats, sitting four to a side rather than five. The wood trim and ceiling finishes are also richer. *Keith Leppard/ Martin Lawrence*

Left: **CARRIAGE WORKS** The oldest railway coaches were made entirely of timber, but by the end of the 19th century underframes were being made of steel, and steel panelling started to be used soon after; body framing switched to steel from the 1950s onwards. No matter how well a steel-panelled coach is cared for, eventually its panelling will need replacement. Here work progresses on re-panelling SR Bulleid Brake 3rd No 2526. Built in 1951, the coach entered traffic on the Bluebell in 2009. *Richard Salmon*

Above: **SOUTHERN RAILWAY No 1309** One of the earliest full carriage restorations at the Bluebell was that of SR Maunsell Open 3rd No 1309, built in 1935. Work was completed in 1984 and earned its restorers the prestigious Association of Railway Preservation Societies' Coach of the Year Award. It has since run almost continuously in public service. *Keith Leppard*

LONDON & SOUTH WESTERN RAILWAY No 1520, a Brake 3rd, was built in 1910 and intended originally to carry passengers and their volumes of luggage on long-distance services. It entered traffic in 2010 in the distinctive salmon and bitter chocolate livery of the LSWR after a 20-year restoration.

Right: **SOUTHERN RAILWAY No 1336,** built in 1933 by Richard Maunsell, provides 3rd Class accommodation in open saloons. With seats trimmed in jazz-pattern moquette, it was returned to traffic in 2008 following more than a decade of work. *Keith Leppard*

Above: Pictured at Kingscote, No 1520 displays a destination board appropriate to its origins; Bude was one of the seaside resorts at the far west of the LSWR route map. *Keith Leppard*

Right: The interior of No 1520 is as striking as the exterior, seen here on its first day in service on 7 August 2010. *Keith Leppard*

Left: **LBSCR BOGIE IST No 7598** Built in 1903, this is the only example at the railway of an LBSCR bogie coach for normal passenger use. Restoration took a decade, including provision of a replacement underframe; it entered service in 1999. Requiring some further work in the late 2000s, it is pictured here in fully lined early SR livery soon after its return to traffic in May 2012. *Keith Leppard*

Left and below: **LBSCR FOUR-WHEEL IST No 661** This was the first four-wheel coach to be restored to use at the railway. Built by Stroudley in 1880, No 661 is from the same era as the railway's 'Terrier' locomotives, *Stepney* and *Fenchurch*. Its coach body had survived since 1924, minus underframe and wheels, incorporated into a house. Representing the previous generation of 1stCclass provision to that offered by No 7598, No 661 entered service at the railway in 2004. It is pictured here in two views from 2007. *Keith Leppard*

Below: **SR SEMI-OPEN BRAKE 3RD No 2526** The Bluebell operates several examples of coaches to designs by O.V. S. Bulleid for the Southern Railway in the 1940s. Considerably more modern than coaches of the previous Maunsell era, their production continued after the 1948 nationalisation and many of their design features were continued in the later BR Standard Mark 1 coaches that also feature in the Bluebell's working fleet. No 2526 entered Bluebell service in 2009 following a lengthy restoration and is pictured at Horsted Keynes in February 2010. The wisp of steam is from a leak in the steam heating system. *Keith Leppard*

Extending North: 1980-1994

Right: **A ROUTE REDISCOVERED** A quarter of a century on from the dismantling of the original line north from Horsted Keynes, the trackbed was so overgrown as to be barely visible in many places, and had structures built on it for farm use in others. Nature had clearly reasserted itself in this view taken at Horsted House farm on 6 May 1989. *Mike Esau*

Left: **NORTH OF LEAMLAND BRIDGE** Thoughts of extending the railway back to East Grinstead began in 1974, when the chance arose to purchase the former West Hoathly station site, but work on the ground only began in 1988 once legal issues had been sorted out and the railway had managed to secure the part of the trackbed immediately north of Horsted Keynes. Here, the railway's Ransoms & Rapier steam crane is in use for the ceremonial start of tracklaying north of Leamland Bridge on 13 March 1988. *Mike Esau*

Right: **HORSTED HOUSE FARM SHUTTLE** Public services over the first mile of the extension to Horsted House Farm bridge began in the spring of 1990. Trains were formed of two 1930s Maunsell carriages, the northern one – a Brake Composite – being adapted to allow 'push-pull' working. SECR 'P' Class locomotive No 323 *Bluebell* is pictured at the then northern limit of the line with the first train on the first full day of operations, 19 May 1990. *Mike Esau*

Left: **THROUGH SHARPTHORNE TUNNEL** To reach West Hoathly, the next target of the extension, the route to and through Sharpthorne Tunnel had to be reinstated. This work was completed in time for No 35027 *Port Line* to break the banner at the official opening of the tunnel on 16 May 1992. With public attention at the time focused on the construction of the Channel Tunnel, it seemed only right that the Bluebell's own version of the 'Golden Arrow' service, which famously linked London and Paris, should have the honour. *Mike Esau*

Right: **NEW COOMBE BRIDGE** A significant gap in the route just north of West Hoathly, where a brick arch underbridge had been demolished after British Railways closed the line, had to be filled for the extension to reach Kingscote. Here one of three spans of a steel girder bridge is craned into position on 10 May 1993 as the push north continues. Trains began running over the last part of the 4 miles from Horsted Keynes to Kingscote on 23 April 1994. *Mike Esau*

Left: **WEST HOATHLY** A temporary run-round loop was provided at West Hoathly so that the regular trains from Sheffield Park could run through to this new terminus, although since no station was established – a condition of the planning consent for the extension – passengers could not alight from the train. SR Class 'S15' No 847 is pictured at this temporary terminus on 22 May 1993. *Bluebell Archive (R. Bamberough)*

Horsted Keynes to Kingscote

LEAMLAND BRIDGE crosses the line at the northern end of the Horsted Keynes station area. With both main and loop lines extending some distance beyond the bridge, the section has the appearance of double track. In this picture, SECR Class 'P' No 178 and Class 'C' No 592 double-head a northbound train formed of SR stock of the Bulleid and Maunsell eras on 21 May 2011. No 178 is the third of the railway's 'P' Class tanks. Unlike No 27 and No 323 *Bluebell*, it had to wait many years before finally being restored and entering service at the railway for the first time in 2010. *Keith Leppard*

HORSTED HOUSE FARM CROSSING
The line continues to climb steeply from Horsted Keynes, leaving behind the river valleys to reach the Wealden plateau. Class 'E4' No B473 makes a fine sight as it heads a northbound train towards Horsted House Farm crossing on 20 February 2010. Next to the locomotive is a six-wheel milk tanker, built in 1933 for express dairy traffic from the West Country to London. Behind it is SECR 3rd Class coach No 1098; built in 1922 for suburban traffic, its 10 compartments are each intended to accommodate 10 passengers (hence the nickname '100-seater'), although this is a tight squeeze – the commuter's lot perhaps hasn't changed so much! *Keith Leppard*

Left: **HORSTED HOUSE FARM BRIDGE** From the footpath crossing, the line enters a cutting that leads to Horsted House Farm occupation bridge, where SECR Class 'C' No 592 is pictured on a very snowy 19 December 2009. *Jon Bowers*

Below left: **BLACK HUT** North of Horsted House Farm bridge, the route follows a series of twists and cuttings that lead to Sharpthorne Tunnel. For many years out of bounds to lineside photographers, this section is not pictured so often as other parts of the route. BR Standard Class 4 No 75027 pilots No 34028 *Eddystone* on a northbound charter in 2006. *Jon Bowers*

Below: **SHARPTHORNE TUNNEL** The railway's 'E4' tank, in BR livery as No 32473, is pictured here on 28 April 2008 leaving the southern portal of the tunnel on another photographers' charter. The leading coaches are in the carmine and cream livery of the early days of British Railways. Commonly known as 'blood and custard', this livery didn't wear well and was later replaced by green on the Southern Region and maroon elsewhere. *Jon Bowers*

WEST HOATHLY At the north end of Sharpthorne Tunnel the line levels out and passes through the site of the former West Hoathly station. This represents a fine vantage point to watch the trains pass.

Right: With the sun high in the west to light up the cutting, GWR 'Dukedog' No 9017 *Earl of Berkeley* heads north with the Metropolitan set on 10 October 2009. Built in 1938 from parts obtained from much older 'Duke' and 'Bulldog' classes, this locomotive came to the Bluebell in 1962 and has since had several periods of service on the line. *Derek Hayward*

Below: Some of the platform-face brickwork is still visible, but most traces of West Hoathly station had gone by the time the railway acquired the site. SR Class 'U' No 1638 storms through with a rake of BR Mark 1 coaches in March 2006. *Paul Pettitt*

Right: **BIRCH FARM CROSSING** From West Hoathly to Kingscote, the northbound gradient is gently falling and the line passes through woodlands with glimpses of the rolling fields beyond. Rebuilt 'Battle of Britain' Class No 34059 *Sir Archibald Sinclair* rounds the curve towards Birch Farm foot crossing with a heavy northbound train on a fine spring day, 26 April 2009. *Derek Hayward*

Left: **BIRCH FARM CROSSING** From Birch Farm there is a short uphill run into Kingscote. No B473 (LBSCR 'E4' Class No 473 in its early Southern Railway livery) is seen here with a matching set of SR carriages heading south past the crossing on 24 October 2010. *Keith Leppard*

Below left: **BIRCHSTONE BRIDGE**, the final overbridge before reaching Kingscote, makes a fine backdrop to views of southbound trains. LBSCR 'A1' No 672 *Fenchurch* is seen here with an Observation Car special in October 2010. Built in 1872, *Fenchurch* is the railway's oldest locomotive. It came to the railway in 1964 and ran in several guises before being rebuilt to its original 'A1' appearance in 2001 for further service. *Dave Bowles*

Below: **KINGSCOTE SIGNAL CABIN** The single-line points are located some distance south of Kingscote station, where the signalman is based in a small cabin. Rebuilt 'Battle of Britain' Class No 34059 *Sir Archibald Sinclair* passes the cabin with a train of BR Mark 1 carriages on 30 April 2011. Built in 1947, this locomotive was originally very similar to No 21C123 *Blackmore Vale* but was rebuilt to a more conventional appearance (and mechanical design) in 1960. *Martin Lawrence*

Wagons and Freight

EARLY MORNING GOODS The Bluebell collection includes many wagons of historic interest as well as some kept primarily to serve the railway's civil engineering needs. Although it carries no freight traffic today, the railway operates demonstration goods trains for the benefit of visitors and photographers, re-creating what was such an important aspect of railway operations. Pictured here on 13 September 2008, SECR centenarians Class 'O1' No 65 and Class 'C' No 592 ascend Freshfield Bank in the early-morning mist. *Dave Bowles*

Below: **HEAVY FREIGHT** The British Railways Class 9F was the ultimate development of UK steam locomotive design for freight haulage, intended for working heavy mineral traffic. Here, the Bluebell's example, No 92240, which was restored from a scrapyard wreck during the 1980s, heads a train of engineering wagons near Ketches Wood in October 2002. *Jon Bowers*

Above: **GOODS IN SPRING** Class 'B4' 0-4-0T No 96 *Normandy* was built by Adams in 1893 for moving freight around the LSWR docks network in Southampton. It has far more power than you would expect from its size, but it is not able to travel easily at line speed, even though this is only 25mph, so is not often used on passenger trains. *Normandy* is seen here heading south past Three Arch Bridge in 2006 on a goods working formed of pre-grouping wagons. *Paul Pettitt*

Above left: **No 3 CAPTAIN BAXTER** This industrial 0-4-0T, built in 1877, worked at a lime works adjacent to Betchworth station in Surrey until it came to the Bluebell in 1960. With its distinctive red livery, *Captain Baxter* is a favourite with younger visitors. Until it was fitted with a vacuum brake in 2012, it was only used for shunting and for hauling demonstration goods trains. It is pictured here just south of Kingscote in August 2010. *Derek Hayward*

Above right: **SECR CLASS 'C' No 592** storms north under Leamland Bridge with a mixed goods working for Kinsgscote on 14 April 2012. 0-6-0 tender engines were the classic British goods locomotive design and the 'C' Class was Wainwright's version of this for the SECR. 109 of them were built in the first decade of the 20th century (No 592 in 1902) and more than half were still at work in 1960, a testament to their success. *Dave Bowles*

Left: **BULLEID 'LIGHT PACIFIC'** No 21C123 *Blackmore Vale* is seen here rounding the curve by Town Place Farm on a freight working during the Giants of Steam event in October 2007. Oliver Bulleid designed these locomotives to have an unusually low axle loading (weight) for their power, intending them to be usable on most of the Southern Railway's routes, not just the main lines. They could therefore be found handling all manner of traffic. Their air-smoothed casing earned them the nickname 'Spamcans' after a brand of tinned meat that was popular at the time. Unfortunately, some of their innovative mechanical features proved less than reliable and about half were eventually rebuilt to the form represented at the Bluebell by No 34059 *Sir Archibald Sinclair*. Although the rebuilds were excellent locomotives, their increased weight reduced their line availability, and they were not allowed west of Exeter. *Derek Hayward*

Right: **PICK-UP GOODS** In the days when every station had a goods yard and the railways were the universal carrier, required by law to carry any goods and parcels on demand, pick-up goods workings featured on any and every branch line. Wending their way from station to station, stopping each time to shunt the yard and pick up or deposit wagons there, these trains certainly took their time to get from A to B. In fine early spring sunshine, SECR 'P' Class No 178 re-creates such a working, approaching Tremains with a northbound mixed goods train on 8 March 2011. *Martin Lawrence*

Left: **ENGINEERS' TRAIN** The low winter sun in February 2010 throws sharp shadows as No 9017 *Earl of Berkeley* takes a lengthy train of engineering wagons, normally used for carrying fresh or spent ballast, north past the abutments of the former Town House Farm occupation bridge, between Freshfield and Monteswood Lane bridges. When the railways were constructed, many bridges had to be provided to connect farmland that had been bisected by the line. Over the years, as the ownership of the land changed, some of these, such as Town House, lost their original purpose, so when the bridge needed expensive repairs in the 1980s the decision was taken to demolish it and devote the money to other capital projects. *Jon Bowers*

Kingscote station

Below: **KINGSCOTE** is about 4 miles north of Horsted Keynes. It is a delightful wayside station with two platforms and a small goods yard, lovingly preserved in the style of the 1950s British Railways period. The atmosphere on Platform 1 is captured in this view taken in March 2011. There is no public parking allowed at Kingscote under the terms of the planning consent for the extended railway. *Keith Leppard*

Right: **WARM WELCOME** At Kingscote, just as at Sheffield Park and Horsted Keynes, a traditional coal fire in the booking hall awaits travellers during a cold November day in 2012. *Martin Lawrence*

Below: **A PLATFORM RE-CREATED** When the railway took over the station site in 1985 it had been in use as a private house. The up platform and main station buildings were largely intact, but the down platform and its buildings had been demolished and the subway filled with rubble. Progressively these were reinstated. This picture shows the recreated down side of the station in July 2012. A train formed of SR coaches stands at the opposite platform. *Keith Leppard*

Right: **COUPLING UP** Between 1994 and 2012, when Kingscote served as the northern terminus of the line, large numbers of passengers periodically disrupted its tranquillity, watching while the locomotives ran around their trains. Here, the crew of 'P' Class No 178 couple up for the journey south in front of an admiring audience. With trains now running on to East Grinstead, Kingscote is a through station again, which passengers visit to enjoy the goods yard display and picnic area, or just to soak up its sleepy charm. *Keith Leppard*

STEAM WATCHING Standing on Kingscote's down platform is one of the best places on the railway to take pictures of the trains from the east side.

Below left: The railway's first locomotive, LBSCR 'A1X' No 55 *Stepney,* a perennial favourite with younger visitors thanks to its inclusion in Rev W. H. Awdry's stories, arrives with the first two of the Metropolitan Railway carriages to be restored, c1999. *Bluebell Archive (James Young)*

Below right: While the driver takes a break, the railway's former LBSCR Class 'E4' tank No B473 sits in the crisp early sunshine on 24 October 2010 alongside a set of SR Maunsell coaches in matching livery. *Keith Leppard*

Extending North: 1994-2013

Below: **CLAY HEADS SOUTH** Having reached Kingscote in 1994, it took another 20 years to complete the final 1.5 miles of the line to East Grinstead. By far the largest obstacle to overcome was the 100,000-ton mountain of domestic rubbish that had been dumped into a deep cutting at Imberhorne during the 1960s. With modern regulations to comply with, its removal represented not just a large physical barrier but also a huge cost. During 2004 tracks were laid from Kingscote up to the southern face of the tip and a considerable amount of inert clay was removed for use elsewhere on the railway. Here, visiting Ivatt Class 2 tank No 41312 is seen departing from the site with the first of these spoil trains on 6 May 2005. *Nigel Longdon*

Right: **EXTENSION SHUTTLE** As part of fundraising to clear the Imberhorne tip, special shuttle trains were run to its southern end using the railway's LNWR Observation Car, built in 1913 to operate on the scenic routes of North Wales. Here SECR 'P' Class No 323 *Bluebell* returns to Kingscote with an extension shuttle in May 2011. This iconic Bluebell locomotive had returned to traffic earlier in the year with its name lettered on its tanks in SECR style in place of its previous brass nameplates. *Keith Leppard*

Below: **THE TRACK STOPPED HERE** A view of the southern tip face under Imberhorne Lane bridge, taken in January 2009, shows the scale of the waste mountain then blocking further progress northwards. The infill continued at the full height of a deepening cutting for 300 metres from here to the Hill Place Farm overbridge. *Nigel Longdon*

Below: **NEW TRACKWORK** Although the first removal of waste from the tip was by road, it proved more efficient to send the material out by rail. To this end, trackwork was completed at the future East Grinstead station and extended southwards over the viaduct to link the northern end of the tip with the national rail network, re-establishing a connection that the railway last enjoyed in 1964. This picture shows the newly installed track at the south end of the station; the Network Rail connection is on the right. A Class 73 locomotive waits on Imberhorne viaduct with the first train of empty wagons for the waste removal operation on 3 July 2010. *Nigel Longdon*

Above: **RUBBISH HEADS NORTH** 1,000-ton train loads of waste from the cutting at Imberhorne departed daily for many weeks during 2011, each one costing about £50,000 to dispatch. This picture, taken in October 2011 from the Hill Place Farm occupation bridge at the northern end of the tip, shows waste being loaded into wagons for one of these trains; it also illustrates very well the industrial scale of the operation. *Gordon Callander*

Arriving at East Grinstead

Below: **EAST GRINSTEAD STATION**
Only a small site was available for a Bluebell Railway station at East Grinstead. Located just south of the station that serves the national rail network, it has a single platform and run-round loop. A water tower is being provided as many of the smaller locomotives will need to take water having made the northbound trip, but all signalling is controlled from Kingscote. Taken on 17 January 2013, this picture shows the Bluebell station with a train on the national network stabled behind the platform. At this time, track panels for the final link through Imberhorne cutting were being assembled at the station, then transported south for use. *John Sandys*

Above: **EAST GRINSTEAD STATION** The new 'running-in' nameboard ready for passengers in September 2010. *Derek Hayward*

Above: **BERNARD HOLDEN MBE** Although Imberhorne cutting remained full of rubbish at the time, the new Bluebell Railway station at East Grinstead was formally opened over the weekend of 4/5 September 2010. On that occasion, the Bluebell Railway Preservation Society's then president, Bernard Holden (seated), was pictured at the station flanked by senior members of the Society. Sadly Bernard passed away in October 2012, so just missed the chance to ride on the first Bluebell steam train to East Grinstead. He had chaired the inaugural meeting of the Society in 1959 and worked with and for the Bluebell Railway throughout its first 50 years. Without him it is hard to imagine that the railway would have survived and flourished as it has. *Derek Hayward*

ARRIVING AT EAST GRINSTEAD After a monumental effort through a long cold winter, the railheads from north and south were finally joined in a ceremony under Imberhorne Lane bridge at the south of the cutting on 8 March 2013. After a further week of ballasting and levelling the track, the first steam locomotive since the closure and dismantling of the line some 50 years earlier finally arrived at East Grinstead from the south on 16 March. Test trains using various locomotives were run over the subsequent days before the public opening the following week. On 21 March 2013 SR Class U No 1638 (left) and SECR Class H No 263 (right) are seen coming off the viaduct and into East Grinstead station on two of these workings. These images depict the culmination of the Bluebell Railway's 40 year northern extension journey and are a testament to the work of so many who made it happen. *Martin Lawrence*

Left: **THEN AND NOW**
No 55 *Stepney* waits at
Sheffield Park on 21 August
1960 – the first season of
operation. *Bluebell Archive
(J. C. Haydon)*

Right: **THEN AND
NOW** BR Standard Class
4 tank No 80151 nears
Horsted Keynes with a
heavily loaded southbound
train on 10 March 2012.
Derek Hayward

Index of Locomotives

3 *Captain Baxter* — 10, 40
4 *Sharpthorn* — 10
W8 *Freshwater* (LBSCR 'A1X' Class) — 26
27 (SECR 'P' Class) — 5
55 *Stepney* (LBSCR 'A1X' Class) — 4, 18, 26, 27, 43, 48
(as BR 32655) — 7
65 (SECR 'O1' Class) — 17, 38
72 *Fenchurch* (LBSCR 'A1X' Class) — 23
(as LBSCR 672) — 1, 3, 11, 23, 26, 27, 37
96 *Normandy* (LSWR 'B4' Class) — 39
178 (SECR 'P' Class) — 9, 10, 27, 34, 41, 43
263 (SECR 'H' Class) — 13, 47
323 *Bluebell* (SECR 'P' Class) — 4, 10, 15, 32, 44
473 *Birch Grove* (LBSCR 'E4' Class) — 5, 11
(as SR B473) — 7, 10, 17, 27, 34, 37, 43
(as BR 32473) — 22, 35

488 (LSWR 0415 Class) — 5, 16
(as BR 30583) — 16
541 (SR 'Q' Class) — 10, 11
592 (SECR 'C' Class) — 14, 27, 34, 35, 38, 40
662 *Martello* (LSBCR 'A1X' Class) — 26
847 (SR 'S15' Class) — 10, 33
928 *Stowe* (SR 'V' Class) — 13
1618 (SR 'U' Class) — 16
1638 (SR 'U' Class) — Cover, 8, 15, 27, 36, 47
2650 (NLR '75' Class, as 58850) — 10
9017 *Earl of Berkeley* (GWR 'Dukedog') — 16
(as BR 9017) — 6, 36, 41
13236 (Class 08 diesel) — 10, 46
21C123 *Blackmore Vale* (SR 'WC' Class) — 21, 26, 40
30064 (SR 'USA' Class) — 13
32424 *Beachy Head* (LBSCR 'H2' Class) — 12

32678 (LBSCR 'A1X' Class) — 26
34007 *Wadebridge* (SR 'WC' Class) — 26
34028 *Eddystone* (SR 'WC' Class) — 18, 26, 35
34059 *Sir Archibald Sinclair* (SR 'BB' Class) — 21, 27, 36, 37
34081 *92 Squadron* (SR 'BB' Class) — 26
35027 *Port Line* (SR 'MN' Class) — 33
41312 (LMS Class 2 tank) — 44
73082 *Camelot* (BR Class 5) — 11, 15
75027 (BR Class 4) — 11, 35
80064 (BR Class 4 tank) — 12
80100 (BR Class 4 tank) — 12
80151 (BR Class 4 tank) — 10, 21, 22, 48
92212 (BR Class 9F) — 10
92240 (BR Class 9F) — 11, 39